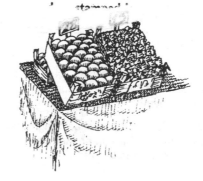

THE
OUTSIDER'S GUIDE
to
HORTICULTURE

1995 Edition

OUTSIDER'S GUIDE

FOREWORD

ACKNOWLEDGEMENTS

Grateful thanks are given to National Westminster Bank PLC for their help and guidance in the structure and content of this publication. National Westminster Bank PLC together with Outsider's Guide, jointly financed the production of the original copy .

In particular, thanks are given to Sally Cottle, Michael Singh, Malcolm Withnal, Rod Mill and Helen Cottle, Steve and Jan Bird all of whom provided significant technical, editorial or artistic contributions to the final copy and layout.

OUTSIDERS GUIDE TO HORTICULTURE 1995

Copyright © Outsider's Guide
1995 Edition published by Outsider's Guide
Ryelands, Stow, Lincoln LN1 2DE. UK Tel: 01427 788 905 Fax: 01427 787 026

ISBN 0 9525061 1 4

While this book has been prepared taking care to provide accurate information, the publisher does not accept any liability whatsoever for any omission or inaccuracy of fact or opinion, or any loss however caused.

Printed and bound by Da Costa Print, Queensland Road, London

OUTSIDER'S GUIDE

FOREWORD

THE OUTSIDER'S GUIDE SERIES

This is just one of the books in the Outsider's Guide series. There are three currently available. These are the Outsider's Guide to Crops, Animals and Horticulture.

The Outsider's Guides were specifically created to meet the need for concise, up-to-date information as a hand book. The Outsider's Guide provides key information about an enterprise in an easy to use and readily accessible layout.

This series is for all those who have not been involved in agriculture on a day to day basis but are about to be, or those that occasionally need to understand the nature of the business of farmers and growers.

Many people from many professions are using the Outsider's Guide. These are bank staff, accountants, agricultural students, journalists, loss adjusters, sales staff of agricultural suppliers, tax inspectors and advisory staff.

The series is an essential reference for every professional providing services to farmers and growers in the United kingdom.

THE OUTSIDER'S GUIDE TO HORTICULTURE

The Outsider's Guide to Horticulture takes a broad view of the Horticultural industry in the United kingdom. This hand book explains the economic environment in which the industry operates, from the effects of the European Union to the influence of major food multiples.

The marketing and distribution systems for getting horticultural produce from grower to consumer is explained for everything from flowers to fruit, and trees to tubers.

The core of this publication takes you through each sector within Horticulture. These sectors are Soft Fruit; Top Fruit; Field Grown and Protected Vegetables; Field Grown and Protected Flowers and Bulbs; Herbaceous and Nursery Stock; Hops and Vines.

On a crop by crop basis you are provided with key facts, seasonal availability from the UK and overseas, together with a husbandry resumé. Finally, for each sector there is a factual and financial summary - everything from investment information to gross margins.

Summarising the major legal trends within the industry, the Outsider's Guide to Horticulture finally leaves you with a list of the major EU Regulations, useful contacts and a horticultural glossary.

OUTSIDER'S GUIDE

HOW TO USE THIS GUIDE

This Guide presents you with four main sections, all but section 3 being general, taking a view of the whole industry. Sections 1 and 2 should be read as background to the Horticultural Industry in the UK while section 4 is there for further reference and an understanding of the special terminology used throughout the industry.

Section 1 - Introduction

Sets the scene for UK Horticulture as part of the whole EU and World Horticultural industry - a factual and political commentary which tries to illustrate the opportunities that the horticultural sector faces in Britain today, as well as the factors that inhibit its development. Read section 1 for an awareness of those topical developments to watch for as the year progresses.

Section 2 - Marketing

Explores outlets and trends for horticultural produce. Of particular interest is the strengthening role of the multiples in determining the future prosperity of the industry in Britain. This section is a lesson for all those entering the sector, stressing the need for a truly commercial approach to any horticultural enterprise - and appreciating the changing demands of the public and those organisations buying produce to meet those demands.

Section 3 - Specialists Sectors

Concerned with individual crop enterprises, section 3 is for all those people who for one reason or another need to find out more about the basic requirements and opportunities for a particular crop. The section looks at each of the commercially important crops. A standard layout is provided for each to enable easy reference.

Where there are many crops within a group, one or two examples only have been selected. This is particularly true for protected flowers and hardy nursery stock which include simply hundreds of 'products' available from garden centres and other outlets.

The pattern followed is as follows:

> Introduction to the crop
> Availability through the year from UK producers
> Availability through the year from overseas producers
> Key Facts*
> Chart of output values**
> Grading Standards - where published
> Husbandry summary
> Production cycle

* Key fact: Information are figures published predominantly by MAFF Basic Horticultural Statistics (July 1994 edition) and the Fresh Produce Desk Book 1994.
** chart This shows trends in output amplified as the vertical axis does not begin at zero.

At the end of a crop group (e.g. Soft Fruit) the financial considerations are summarised along with original gross margin tables derived especially for the Outsider's Guide.

The horticultural crop groups discussed in this Outsider's Guide are as shown below:

A. Soft Fruit		Strawberries, Raspberries, Blackcurrants, Gooseberries.
B. Top Fruit		Dessert Apples, Culinary Apples, Pears, Plums, Cherries.
C. Vegetables	Field grown	Legumes (Runner Beans, Dwarf or French) , Brassicas (Brussels Sprouts, Calabrese, Cabbage, Chinese Cabbage, Cauliflower), Roots (Carrots, Onions - Dry Bulb and Green), Leeks, Asparagus, Celery, Iceberg Lettuce, Watercress.
D. Vegetables	Protected	Mushrooms, Cucumbers, Tomatoes (heated and cold), Celery, Butterhead Lettuce.
E. Flowers & Bulbs	Field - flowers	Narcissi, Gladioli
	Field - bulbs	Tulips, Narcissi
F. Flowers & Plants	Protected	Chrysanthemums, Carnations, Pot Plants (flowering and foliage), Bedding Plants.
G. Nursery Stock		Alpines, Herbaceous, Heathers, Roses, Shrubs and Trees.
H. Beverage Crops		Hops, Vines and Cider Apples

Section 4 - Regulations, Contacts and Terms

This begins with a brief look at what is happening as far as EU regulations will affect the industry and those within it. 'Contacts' is a list of a large number of useful organisations which are associated with crops described in this publication. Of course, there are many more than those listed, but it will serve as a starting point for further study or research into any particular enterprise type. Finally, the glossary explains all the common horticultural terms used in the industry.

CONTENTS

OUTSIDER'S GUIDE

CONTENTS

OUTSIDER'S GUIDE

CONTENTS

THE HORTICULTURAL INDUSTRY

INTRODUCTION

YOUR NOTES

Use this page (there's one available at the start of every section), to make any notes that you require to help you in your work. These notes may be references to pages in this section or within the whole book which are useful to you, or additional information which the Outsider's Guide has not included.

OUTSIDER'S GUIDE

Considerable structural changes in both the consumption and sale of fruit and vegetables has taken place in the last thirty years, and these trends are set to continue to the end of the century. European Union (EU) policies and the horticultural production from other member states also offers major challenges and opportunities for UK growers. Beyond the EU, our markets are open to producers anywhere in the world.

The sector therefore, has to be highly competitive and this Guide aims to set out the economic and management environment of the industry. This Guide will be an aid to investors, lenders, growers and all those who want to understand the nature, scope and variety of UK horticulture.

THE EUROPEAN UNION

Currently, the fruit and vegetable sector represents 16% of agricultural output of the EU, with 1.8 million farm families depending on what is a very labour-intensive industry. Clear differences are distinguishable between different regions of the Union, with fruit and vegetables making up 27% of final agricultural production in Spain, 27% in Italy, 23% in Greece - more than double the comparable figures in most northern member states.

Income of fruit-growing holdings are above average in the north, but below average in southern EU states. The EU remains one of the world's biggest importers of fruit and vegetables, with imports totalling ECU 1.95 billion every year. The trade deficit in the sector is estimated at ECU 1.28 billion. This represents an opportunity for all producers.

THE UNITED KINGDOM

The Retail Sector

The market for fruit and vegetables, once the preserve of small growers and retailers, is now dominated by the multiple sector which commands 51% of the volume in each category. Greengrocers now account for 23% of fruit and 22% of vegetables whilst retail markets with 13% and 10% respectively remain important outlets.

Consumer Trends

The emphasis on healthy eating and ease of preparation and convenience has also contributed towards the growth of the multiple sector and changes in consumption. Sales of fresh produce such as cabbage, Brussels sprouts and root vegetables has declined in importance compared to more user-friendly produce such as courgettes and tinned and frozen equivalents. More adventurous consumer taste has also led to an increasing demand for more exotic varieties of fruit and vegetables.

Trade Deficit

These trends have greatly contributed to Britain's total food and drink deficit which amounted to £5.5 billion in 1991. Valued at £260 per household per year, the deficit includes

---

EU POLICY

£1.7 billion for fruit and £0.9 billion for vegetables. 'Food From Britain' began a campaign in 1990 aimed at assisting both sectors to reduce these deficits.

Why a Deficit?

Fruit and vegetable deficits result from both the importation of produce which cannot be grown in the UK and significantly, the import of items of which more could be grown in the UK. The current absence of any major exports in either sector ensures that there is little scope to offset the cost of imports.

Future Changes

Political changes across the world in recent years will continue to have a major impact on world trade and this will increasingly affect the UK horticultural market.

THE EUROPEAN DIMENSION

The European Union will be enlarged in 1995 with the accession of the former EFTA members, Sweden, Finland, and Austria. These countries are unlikely to pose a significant threat to the UK but will provide improved access for UK produce. Beyond 1995, Cyprus, Malta and Turkey are still intent on EU membership and former Eastern Bloc states such as Poland, Hungary and the Czech Republic are aiming to become members before the end of the decade.

The EU Fruit & Vegetable Regime

Rene Steichen - EU Farm Commissioner - outlined in September 1994 the future of the EU fruit and vegetable sector. The essentials involve no reduction of EU expenditure, currently running at ECU 1.6 million, but aim to target this more effectively. New policy objectives are:

1. Better grouping of supplies to match increasingly concentrated distribution chains.
2. A new way of managing short-term surpluses.
3. Gradual elimination of structural surpluses; creating a better balance between fresh and processed product; redefining standards.
4. Introducing specific measures for those products not covered by particular regimes, and introducing more stringent control methods.

The current regime has been closely orientated to the market situation and proved the effectiveness of a decentralised management system. Existing arrangements could be improved by:

1. Strengthening the role of producer organisations.
2. Reducing the attraction of market withdrawals.

3. Improving quality standards.

4. Broadening the amount of data available.

The Commission rejects the idea of quotas or of an area payment on a per hectare basis as being potentially damaging to the "dynamism" of the sector.

Community Preference Safeguarded

Community preference will not be jeopardised, despite the various GATT commitments on imports. The most pressing problem facing the fruit and vegetable sector post-Uruguay Round will be to set up instruments to ensure the respect of the entry price system which will replace the current preference price arrangements.

THE WORLD DIMENSION

The scene beyond Europe is perhaps a potential threat for the UK. Two major fruit producers in South Africa and Chile now enjoy increased access to world markets with the restoration of democratic governments in these countries. Despite the promise of improved trading relations across the world as result of the GATT Uruguay Round, the UK will continue to find markets beyond Europe difficult to penetrate, and particularly the newly formed trading bloc in North America comprising the USA, Canada and Mexico.

UK Disadvantaged

'Food From Britain' has undertaken extensive surveys of both the fruit and vegetable sectors and concluded that the UK is at a distinct disadvantage particularly in relation to European competitors. Climate and the relative shortness of the UK growing season are obvious problems which cannot be significantly changed, but there are key areas where the UK could benefit from structural changes to both sectors. The key areas where change is required are detailed below.

Research

Much less research is being undertaken in the horticultural sector and this will erode further the UK's competitive position. One area of research identified by 'Food From Britain' as particularly important was the need to develop varieties to extend the season so that customers may have fresh produce for longer, and packhouses can operate more economically.

Increase Production

Particularly where fruit is concerned, there is a need to increase production. Despite increasing production, the UK has one of the lowest shares of land area devoted to fruit production in the EU. An increase in fruit production would improve self-sufficiency, reduce fruit sector imports and allow export structures to be developed. For this to occur requires

OPPORTUNITIES

both a re-appraisal of government involvement and re-assessment of current market organisation.

Government Support

A number of our EU competitors enjoy various tax concessions and other government support mechanisms denied to the UK sector. In France for instance a new structural fund has been established to support the beleaguered fruit and vegetable sector. The new fund which is worth £5 million will aim to organise production more effectively and tailor it to the demands of the market. It will also support an aggressive trading policy in order to acquire new markets for French produce.

Most countries also have some form of para-fiscal tax on producers in order to generate promotional funds, the UK by comparison is entirely voluntary. Except where apples and pears are concerned, no organisation exists to co-ordinate such a campaign. There is little doubt that a statutory levy would assist the industry to fund structural changes to improve organisation and marketing.

FUTURE PROSPECTS & OPPORTUNITIES - UK

Global warming apart, the climate in the UK is unlikely to improve sufficiently to aid the horticultural sector. However, there appears to be a growing understanding of the problems faced by the horticultural sector in the UK, and a growing willingness amongst all sectors of the industry to improve British performance. This is reflected in the following developments.

1. Government Aids

The Government has recently introduced a £10 million food marketing scheme aimed at improving the efficiency of the UK food chain by helping farmers, growers and processors to improve their marketing and commercial expertise.

This scheme supersedes the MAFF Marketing Grant Scheme and is open to applications from a wide range of those involved in agriculture, horticulture and food marketing. This includes groups promoting collaboration between producers, individual farmers and food processors or manufacturers with a turn-over of less than £10 million.

Grants   A 50% grant is available towards the cost of projects approved under the scheme, with an upper limit of £150,000 grant per project. Projects must represent a significant marketing development and sufficient scale within the market concerned.

Feasibility study   The NFU has already submitted an application to fund a feasibility study. The study will include market research activity among the existing marketing groups in the main sectors of the horticultural industry. Application forms and additional information on the scheme are available from MAFF on telephone number 0171 238 6600 (fax: 0171 238 6728).

OUTSIDER'S GUIDE

2. Consumer Support

Support / Trends | There is a growing awareness in the UK of the need to support domestic producers. Consumers are developing a taste for British pears in particular, and are buying more English pears and apples. Increasing consumption of produce such as peppers and aubergines also provides UK growers with opportunities to switch production from sectors where the market is saturated, to these types of products which have little history of UK production. Not only would this reduce dependence on imports of these products but could provide important export opportunities.

3. Support of the Multiples

Choose British | Almost two thirds of all tomatoes, cucumbers and lettuces consumed in the UK are sold through supermarkets. The multiples hold the whip hand and in it the destiny of the £154 million sector. A policy of choosing British rather than the cheapest, would give a much needed boost of confidence to home suppliers. Three key British multiples recently expressed their policy on this issue as follows:

Safeway | Safeway has made a 'firm pledge' to buy British whenever possible as part of its involvement in the Strathclyde Food Project. Massive import substitution in all areas has led to increased UK supplies. Virtually all cucumbers and 80 per cent of fresh tomatoes (April to October) are sourced in the UK.

Sainsbury | Sainsbury says it is encouraging growers to extend the UK growing season but when the UK growers have insufficient product to meet demand, are forced to buy imported produce.

Tesco | Tesco says that it pays a premium for UK produce to encourage product innovation but argues that over-supply is pushing prices down.

4. Horticultural Industry Study

Junior farm minister, Michael Jack, recently completed a personal study on the horticultural industry, concluding that there is a real desire by all the multiples to source from home produce whenever they can. In an upbeat assessment of the sector the minister identified the following areas as essential to the overall improvement of the industry:

- business skills
- market intelligence
- promotional activity
- wholesale markets
- export opportunities
- communication of research and development

OPPORTUNITIES

Fruit monitoring

Most of these areas are now being addressed with reference to 'market intelligence'. 1994/95 will be the first UK top fruit season where growers will be monitoring fruit in orchards throughout the regional growing areas. This will help them compile accurate and immediate market information on quality and supply, and to check on fruit destined for winter storage.

5. NFU Support

NFU lobbying on a range of horticultural crops has prompted an inquiry into the UK horticultural industry by the House of Commons Agriculture Select Committee. The NFU has asked that the following issues in particular are addressed:

- undermining of the glasshouse sector in England and Wales
- EU over-production
- high volume of imports from non-EU countries
- government commitment to UK production.

6. Export Opportunity

Continental
challenge

The accessibility of the European market has been greatly enhanced with the opening of the Channel Tunnel. This link is supported by the Continental Challenge initiative, launched in January 1994 by MAFF to highlight export opportunities in Europe. The 'Food From Britain' Group are also holding a series of regional seminars to help exporters achieve tangible results.

Ministry's
E.R.T.P

The Ministry's Market Task Force, together with its External Relations and Trade Promotion Division are ready to advise on exporting. They can be contacted on 0171 238 5642 and 0171 270 8148 respectively.

Export grant

The relatively immature markets of Eastern Europe offer excellent export opportunities for UK producers. For example, a company known as Salads Etceteras Holdings have been awarded a Ministry of Agriculture export grant to develop the Eastern European market for British salads produce. The group is one of the largest suppliers of cucumbers to the multiples with a turnover in excess of £16 million.

Like other companies expansion will be into Europe and CIS aiming at a market of 350 million people. Exports will include early season English cucumbers, iceberg lettuces, tomatoes, cabbages and carrots which are often in short supply between February and May, given a hard winter and relatively poor storage facilities in Poland.

There are, despite climatic problems, a number of opportunities for British producers to help cut the current UK deficit in both fruit and vegetables. Importantly, the key groups in each sector are working more closely together and this can only augur well for the future.

OUTSIDER'S GUIDE

KEY FACTS - CROP GROWING AREAS UK

This part of the introduction provides an overview of production areas for the main crops or groups of crops, where the crop accounts for more than 5% of the total area grown in the UK. All figures are in hectares and are based on the Ministry of Agriculture's 1992 Census for England and Wales and the Provisional results for Scotland's June 1993 census. (Source 'The Grower: Reference Special '94'.

SOFT FRUIT

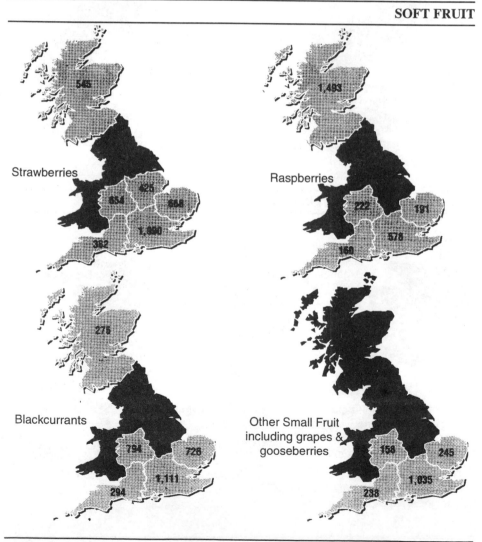

Strawberries

Raspberries

Blackcurrants

Other Small Fruit including grapes & gooseberries

TOP FRUIT

TOP FRUIT

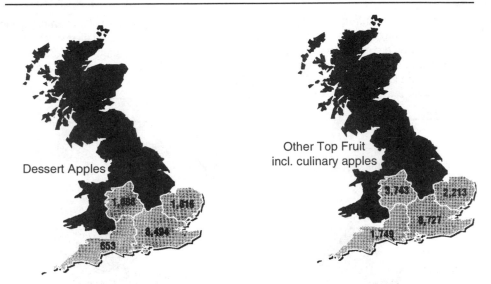

Dessert Apples

Other Top Fruit
incl. culinary apples

FIELD GROWN VEGETABLES

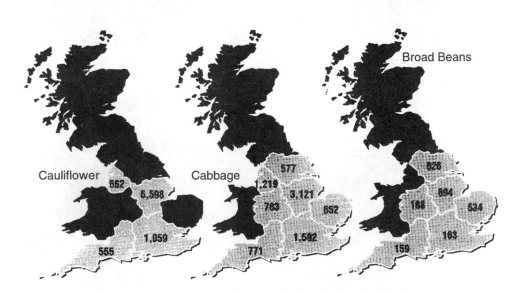

Broad Beans

Cauliflower

Cabbage

OUTSIDER'S GUIDE

FIELD VEGETABLES

FIELD GROWN VEGETABLES

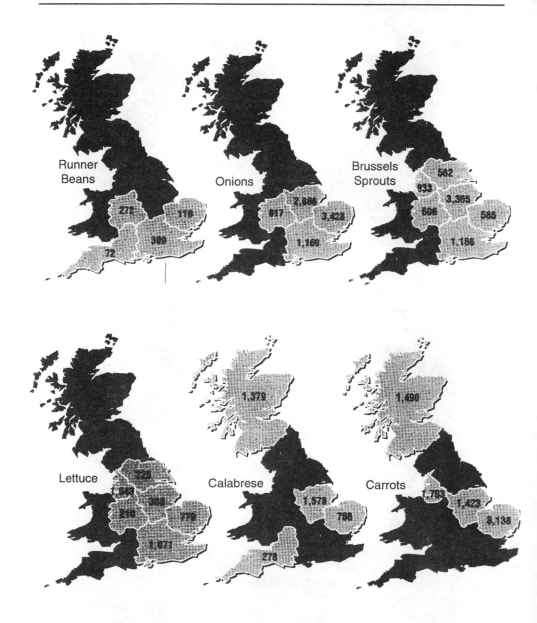

VEGETABLES

PROTECTED VEGETABLES

Cucumbers
90.25
101.63

Tomatoes incl. unheated
57.12
76.49
33.37
28.93
168.25
32.72

Mushrooms
6.34
6.27
5.95
3.08
9.58
22.49
7.42

Lettuce Protected
41.01
32
9.88
13.71
46.15
9.02

FLOWERS & BULBS

FIELD GROWN FLOWERS & BULBS

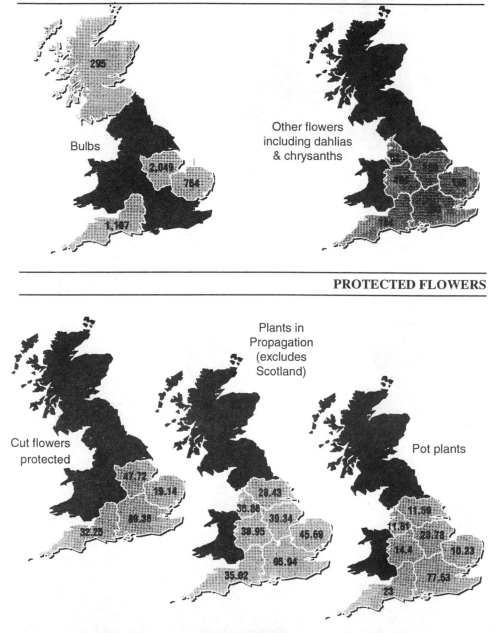

Bulbs

295

2,049

764

1,197

Other flowers
including dahlias
& chrysanths

PROTECTED FLOWERS

Cut flowers
protected

47.72

19.14

89.38

32.75

Plants in
Propagation
(excludes
Scotland)

28.43

38.86

39.34

38.95

45.60

95.94

35.02

Pot plants

11.59

11.51

28.78

14.4

10.23

77.53

23

NURSERY STOCK

NURSERY STOCK

Hardy nursery stock

442
547
770
1,112
1,810
2,332
607

THE HORTICULTURAL INDUSTRY

MARKETING

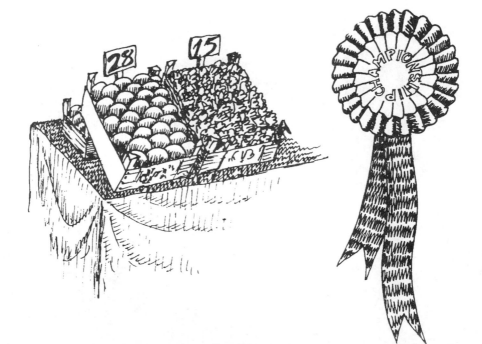

NOTES

HORTICULTURAL MARKETING

This section considers the marketing of horticultural produce. After a brief introduction to the market place and the European situation, this section is divided into four further sub sections. It concludes with an overview of the quality and grading standards. The complete structure is as follows:

1. **The Market Place**
2. **Produce Outlets**
3. **Distribution Channels**
4. **Commodity Review**
5. **Quality & Grading Standards**

Introduction

The horticultural industry, contrary to a commonly held view, is not a small and intensive sector of agriculture - it is in its own right, a very large industry generating almost18% of all agricultural output and over 40% of the agricultural crop output. The annual output of about £1.5 - £2.0 billion is significant to the economy and makes a major contribution to the quality of life of the nation.

Horticultural suppliers have had to be responsive to change. The major changes in the pattern of demand have come from:

- ☞ the emergence of the supermarket or multiple food retailers in the edible sector of horticulture

- ☞ the development of garden centres and containerised plants in the non-edible sector

- ☞ the changes in the 'lifestyle' of consumers and an increasing percentage of women in the work force leading to a reduction in the time available for food preparation; an increase in 'eating out' or take-away meals

- ☞ a public which is more 'health conscious and environmentally aware' and seeking new interests in its leisure time

THE MARKET PLACE

Traditionally, horticulture has not received government price support since joining the European Union (EU). The sector is fully exposed to the disciplines of the supply and demand aspects of marketing in a free market. However, a few commodities (apples, cauliflowers) are eligible for intervention payments.

OUTSIDER'S GUIDE

EUROPE

The British horticultural industry within the EU is constantly battling for its market share with the Dutch, French and recently the Spanish. This will continue as the climatic difference between north and south Europe polarise producers costs such as energy, transport and labour, and impact on competitiveness in the market place.

European Legislation

Overburdening of the industry with bureaucracy both due to European Union and home legislation and its implementation, has constrained and inhibited horticulturists in the market place.

Fiscal policy, and the political change in attitude towards farmers and growers in the context of European 'surpluses' and the Common Agricultural Policy, have all reduced the full commercial potential of the industry.

Overseas Competition

The following table illustrates the European situation. Any UK producer must be aware of these sources of competition.

Total Fruit Production ('000 tonnes) 1992/3

Country	Total	Apples	Pears	Cherries/ Plums	Strawberries	Other Soft Fruit
Italy	1093	2332	997	281	189	294
France	3284	2462	368	302	95	57
Germany	2124	*700	470	643	55	256
Spain	1818	853	459	188	243	75
Holland	438	363	84	7	26	3
UK	443	278	34	23	52	53
Greece	412	267	91	38	6	10
Bellux	367	231	81	23	28	4
Portugal	145	74	41	20	3	7
Denmark	74	45	4	12	9	4
R of Ireland	16	10	n/a	n/a	5	1
Total	13259	7615	2629	1540	711	764

* Excluding Juicing

This chart shows as an example, those fruits which can be produced in UK and the countries from where they are imported.

Total Fruit Production ('000 tonnes) 1992/3

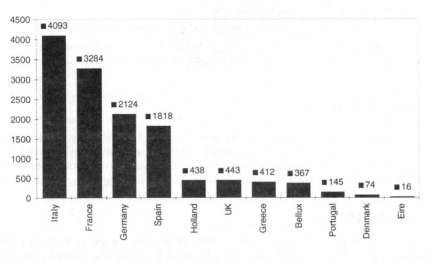

British Production

The changes in demand have brought about a specific response from the suppliers - the growers. Their response has all been designed to improve the quality, quantity and extended availability of products and to enable growers to compete on the basis of specification and cost of production.

Advanced Technology

British horticulturists are amongst the most technically developed in the world:

i) The glass house sector features high technology associated with environmental control.

ii) Many crops are grown in 'soil-less' conditions, using rockwool or nutrient film techniques.

iii) Fruit stores are controlled by computers to exacting levels of temperature and gas concentration.

iv) Irrigation and plant feeding systems are controlled to a high specification.

v) Grading equipment in the packhouse can automatically grade tomatoes and apples by size, colour and quality

vi) Sophisticated 'icebank' coolers have been developed for 'cool-chain' marketing.

SALES OUTLETS

Plant Breeding

i)   Plant breeding and clonal selection have improved a whole range of existing plant lines, particularly in seeking pest and disease resistance.

ii) Tree fruit production has centred on dwarf trees planted at high densities, giving early yield from easily managed trees.

iii) Strawberries are now available for almost six months of the year.

iv) Methods of biological control and integrated pest management have enabled a steady reduction in the use of pesticides across all crops.

---

1. PRODUCE OUTLETS

One stop shopping, out of town parking, and an 'open all hours' policy, has changed the nation's shopping habits. Well graded and presented fresh fruits and vegetables are available year round. Suppliers are required to supply within product specifications, employing strict codes of practice associated with food hygiene, and providing assurances of quality second to none worldwide.

A. Multiple Food Retailers

The major supermarkets have 50% - 55% of the market share in fresh produce. Sainsbury, Tesco, Safeway, Waitrose, Asda, Marks & Spencer, and Gateway are a few of the multi-billion pound turnover British retailing businesses.

Global Market

The enormous scale of their operations positions them as the market's main buyers, whether from the home industry, the Dutch Auction system or the large French and Spanish co-operatives.

Indeed, the multiples operate in what is termed the 'global market' when sourcing supplies. As masters of retailing they are also committed to product development, whether from flavour and taste, packaging or novelty, and seek ever demanding ways of optimising their profits/sq.m of shelf space.

Supported by sophisticated 'composite depots' networked nationwide, involving 'cool chain' distribution, and EPOS product scanning using bar codes, multiples are fast moving, and demanding customers to supply.

The Response of Suppliers

The horticultural industry, is primarily made up of many smaller family businesses. These small businesses have had to join forces to supply these powerful customers from central storage, grading, packing and distribution centres. Grower co-operatives, importer packhouses, independent/merchant packing distribution depots, have all emerged in response to the strength of the multiples.

SALES OUTLETS

Price Erosion

Whilst prices paid to growers have always reflected the quality and service provided, the current High Street 'war' for supremacy amongst the 'big five' has driven prices down to reduce profitability that will, in some sectors, inevitably stop investment in future supplies.

B. The Traditional Wholesale Market

The network of national markets centred on the major conurbations exist today to serve a large proportion of the horticultural industry. There are about 1,000 fruit and vegetable wholesalers handling 40% - 45% of fresh produce sales - down from 80% twenty years ago. However, the buyers using them have changed dramatically. The number of independent grocers/fruiterers has declined, but the street traders and market stall holders remain.

Key Buyers

Specialist retailers, hotels and restaurants, and the catering industry are significant buyers in the wholesale market, taking nearly 50% of the market volume, valued at £1.1 billion annually. The multi-outlet food sector - The National Health Service, fast food chains, contract caterers, school kitchens etc. - involves centralised buying and dedicated distribution.

Product Quality

Products sent to the wholesale market must comply with statutory grading standards embracing Class 1, 2 and 3 standards. However, the 'policing' of compliance to grading standards is not as strict as the multiple depot (renowned for its vigilant quality control).

Declining Market Share of Wholesalers

It is generally acknowledged that there are only a few buyers dealing with numerous suppliers in today's wholesale market. It is anticipated that unless this sector reduces in size and modernises its 100 year-old system of trading, it will lose further market share, and go into a severe decline.

C. Other Outlets, including Processing

Growth in Direct Selling

A small, but significant growth area for horticulture has been direct selling through farm shops, pick your own and ex-nursery sales (packhouse door, and van). Fruit and vegetable growers near large populations or busy roads have capitalised on the public seeking 'fresh produce in the fresh air', and developed out of town shopping centres on a par with the mini-supermarket. Direct sales have a 12% market share.

Co-operatives and Packhouses

Larger packhouses and grower co-operatives have been able to serve processors with economic volumes of supply. In some cases specialist pre-packed products have been developed to meet the demand for 'semi-prepared' vegetables or salads.

PRODUCT TRENDS

The deep freeze and the increased use of the microwave has had a powerful impact on the presentation of certain vegetables. More than 50% of all vegetables go to the processing industry, whether for freezing, canning, pickling or chilling. Peas, beans, carrots and beetroot are the main commodities.

D. The Garden Centre and Floristry Trade

The dual explosion of garden centres and container grown plants have revolutionised the 'non-edible' sector of horticulture. Together they have provided convenience and pleasure to plant buying - easy to park, easy to transport, open during leisure time.

Factors in Demand

i) The emergence of increased home ownership has placed value on homes and gardens, which when combined with the recognition of an improved quality of life and environment, has created an enormous demand.

ii) With further value placed within the community via Local Authorities on amenity provision - parks and gardens, plus provision of open spaces and sports facilities, demand for trees and plants has increased.

iii) Television, gardening magazines, flower festivals and The Chelsea Flower Show, have all contributed to heightened awareness, and stimulated demand.

iv) The traditional celebrations of Christmas, Mother's Day and Easter have stimulated demand in addition to the normal patterns of marriage, birth and death.

v) Colour television and an awareness of the need to improve the home and working environment have stimulated sales of foliage plants.

vi) Dried, silk and quality plastic flowers have further extended the use of plant material.

Product Trends

☛ **Bedding Plants:** One sector of particular growth has been the bedding plant industry, where improved packaging and presentation have met the need for 'instant' colour.

☛ **DIY Stores:** Large DIY chains and multiple stores (Homebase, Texas, B&Q) have moved to the plant supply market and are expanding rapidly.

☛ **Cut Flower Industry:** Allied to garden centres and multiples has been the emergence of the pot plant and cut flower industry.

The garden centre is diverse in type, ranging from the specialist plant centre to the out-of-town leisure centre. It is estimated that there are between 2500 - 2700 such centres. Notcutts, Hilliers, Wyevale, Country Gardens are but a few nationwide. Several of these are primary producers, achieving a high level of vertical integration. Many belong to The Horticultural Trades Association, the promotional body for the gardening industry.

GARDEN CENTRES

Garden centres are selling conservatories, swimming pools and garden sheds, koi carp, pet supplies and garden machinery, in addition to the usual range of plants and horticultural sundries. Many have become sophisticated retail businesses attracting large numbers of visitors for several hours of leisure time. Huge car parks, refreshment areas, including toilets and childrens play areas, enable garden centres to rival other 'tourist' attractions in many areas.

Purchases from Garden Centres 1993

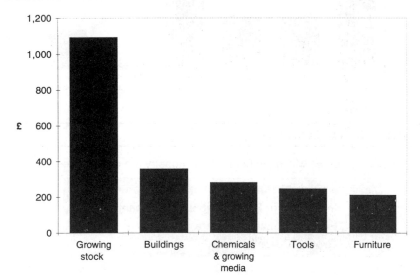

	Total Spent '93	% Sales	
		1988	1993
Growing Stock (including seeds, bedding & pot plants)	£1,096m	33.0	42.0
Buildings	£360m	15.0	14.0
Chemicals (including growing media)	£280m	11.5	10.5
Tools	£250m	11.0	9.5
Furniture	£210m	9.0	8.0

Total garden products expenditure in 1993 is estimated at £2.6 billion

DISTRIBUTION

Garden Centre Share of the Market for some Product Groups (%)

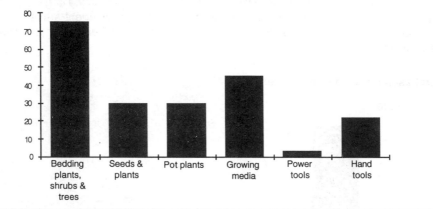

---

2. DISTRIBUTION CHANNELS

The distribution routes within the horticultural industry are mainly via:-

> **A. Grower Packhouses**
>
> **B. Independent Packhouse and Merchant**
>
> **C. Fresh Produce Importers**
>
> **D. Grower Co-operatives**

A. Grower Packhouses

Whether independent or co-operative, all are required to comply to exacting standards of food hygiene. To serve the multiple, additional standards are necessary, including well documented quality assurances. There is a trend towards a reduction of registered packhouses by the multiples.

In many sectors of horticulture too much capital is tied up in resources that have limited operational periods each year. However they are versatile, flexible and responsive.

Horticulture does feature some very large enterprises with their own packhouses e.g. J.J. Barker Ltd (vegetables) and Paynes Fruit Growers in Kent, Hilliers and Notcutts Nurseries in Hants and Suffolk, and Van Heyningen Bros., (salads & part of the Hillsdown Group) in Sussex, and L.O. Jeffs in Lancashire (salads).

SOFT FRUIT

B. Independent Packhouse/Merchant

Growers supply ungraded products to a centralised facility. Volume, range of product and continuity of supply are the features of this channel. The merchant is widely sourcing and has a wide number of outlets.

C. Fresh Produce Importers

There are many large companies in this sector, often dedicated to serving multiples with a range of fresh produce year round. Their procurement divisions source from every country worldwide, and at times are in conflict with home producers. Companies like Geest plc, the Albert Fisher Group, The Mac Organisation and Superior International, supply multiple composite depots direct, or serve wholesale panelists countrywide.

D. Grower Co-operatives

The horticultural industry is well represented in certain sectors for its effective co-operative marketing ventures. Each sector has its notable examples: ENFRU Ltd in the fruit industry; FARGRO Ltd in the nursery stock sector; Bedfordshire Growers Ltd in vegetables; Kentish Garden Ltd in the strawberry industry and Home Grown Salads Ltd in the protected crops sector.

Many are offering a year round service, utilising imported products out of the home season i.e. southern hemisphere fruits, Spanish and Israeli salads and soft fruit.

3. MARKETING - A COMMODITY REVIEW

This sub-section is a snapshot of fruit, vegetable and flower sectors all of which, and more, are discussed in far greater detail in the Specialist Sectors part of this Outsider's Guide.

A. Soft Fruit (strawberries, raspberries, blackcurrants, gooseberries)

Trends	75% of the estimated 10-12,000 hectares of "pick your own" is soft fruit, taking a 10%-12% market share.
Areas	Kent is the main producing county for strawberries, and the Tayside region of Scotland the main raspberry area.
Technology	Glass, French tunnels, cloches and floating covers are used to extend the season.
Products	Blackcurrants are now grown exclusively under contract to processors (Beechams for Ribena) and are harvested mechanically. Other berries, red and white, gooseberry and blackberry are very labour intensive and expensive to pick. The main outlets are to freezers and processors. Raspberries are

TOP FRUIT

also in demand from the multiples. Autumn fruiting varieties (Autumn Bliss) have extended the season.

Outlets   Over 70% of the strawberry crop is marketed in June/July, but an extended season is being developed using improved varieties.

The supermarket's share of the soft fruit market (mostly strawberries) is growing steadily (25%-30%). 'Cool-chain' marketing, and better varieties (Elsanta and Evita) have improved shelf life. Co-operative marketing organisations (Kentish Garden, Kent Fruit) have contributed to market development.

Notes   The development of soft fruits in the market is closely linked to the availability of seasonal pickers, many of whom come as students from Eastern European countries. It is from this geographical area that major competition is envisaged in the future (Hungary, Poland, Romania).

The Spanish strawberry industry enjoys a market dominance from March to May, and has contributed to developing the market prior to the start of the English season.

B. Top Fruit (apples, pears, plums, cherries)

Trends   Imports of French dessert apples in the home season continue to erode the market share of UK producers (now less than 50%), reflecting the supermarkets' increased market share (60-65%) and requirements for uniform, well graded produce.

The cropping area has declined by almost 33% in the past decade. However orchard intensification, with improved output/hectare, has maintained annual production of around 100,000 tonnes of Cox's Orange Pippin and 120,000 tonnes of Bramley.

Areas   Kent is the major fruit growing county, followed by Essex, Suffolk, Sussex and Herefordshire. Cherry and plum production are in decline, although in the Vale of Evesham a renewed interest has resulted in new plantings of plums.

Products   The culinary apple variety Bramley, has a static market, although processing takes 35% of production for pie fillings, apple products, juices and ciders. With less time spent in the kitchen fewer pies and puddings are being 'home prepared'.

There are few indications that the industry wishes to lose its dependence on Cox and Bramley, although Jonagold and Gala clones are being planted. Conference dominates the pear sector, although a new introduction, Concorde, looks promising and is being planted.

OUTSIDER'S GUIDE

Within the EU's annual production potential of 10-12 million tonnes of dessert apples the UK is a small part. With European consumption around 8-9 million tonnes there is a structural surplus of apples, marginalising anything but Class 1 fruit in the market.

Outlets

In 1994 the industry's two largest co-operatives combined to form The English Fruit Company, ENFRU Ltd, to represent 50-55% of the UK supply. Over 65% of all fruit is marketed via co-operatives in the UK. With a more managed supply, plus the promotional efforts and market intelligence information of English Apples and Pears Ltd., it is hoped that it can hold its current market share in the future.

The voluntary promotion of Cox on television has used funds of between £750,000 and £1m in recent years to heighten awareness of the product.

Notes

Early frost and mid summer rains are the barriers to regular cropping and marketing.

The Gro-Act Scheme introduced recently requires grower compliance to a quality assurance schedule directly linked to approved pesticide use. The industry is supported by a retail surveillance scheme monitored by the Women's Farming Union.

Fruit Sales as a % of all Sales

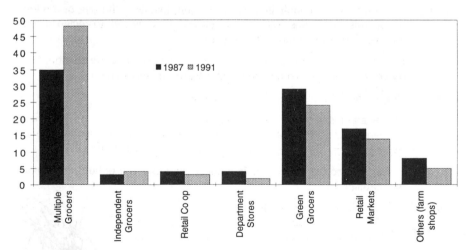

FIELD VEGETABLES

C. Field Grown Vegetables

Trends   Fresh vegetable consumption has remained static, despite innumerable campaigns promoting healthier lifestyles.

However, frozen and processed vegetables have increased by 47% in the last ten years, hand-in-hand with freezer and microwave ownership by busy parents, together with faster foods like pizzas and burgers.

80% of vegetables consumed are either cabbages, carrots, cauliflowers, beans, sprouts, onions or peas. Multiples, processors and the catering industry are the main outlets.

Areas   Vegetable production on arable farms now represents 80% of the total production area, with by far the largest concentration in Eastern England (Lincolnshire, Cambridgeshire and Norfolk).

The traditional market gardener has declined, although specialist units exist in the traditional growing areas (Thames Valley, Kent, Evesham, Lancashire). Many are part of grower co-operatives providing both high volume and continuity of supply to the market.

The UK is 85-90% self sufficient.

Technology   High levels of mechanisation are practiced, involving the use of modular transplants, herbicides and irrigation. Crop agronomy is very precise to meet the exacting requirements of customers.

Plastic fleece crop covers are now widely used to extend the season. Field harvesting rigs (almost mobile packhouses) are very common.

Products   Bulb onions are the largest imported crop.

There are many other diverse crops grown i.e. sweet corn, Chinese cabbage, courgettes, calabrese, watercress, and mange tout peas. Herbs, asparagus, garlic, endives and gherkins are all grown in the UK.

Outlets   Produce Export Services Ltd. is a successful exporter of beetroot, onions and cauliflower.

Organic Production

Trends   Productive area has seen a marked increase in recent years.

Areas   It is estimated about 15,000 hectares are registered with the Soil Association, with a value in excess of £120 million (estimated £18m in 1988).

Products   Mostly vegetables, some fruit crops.

PROTECTED SALADS

Technology	Growers are employing integrated pest management techniques, utilising biological control, and considerable reductions in pesticides applied using modern application methods, to significantly reduce the dependence on chemicals for crop production.
Outlets	Over 10% is sold through the 'big five' supermarkets, Sainsbury, Tesco and Safeway being the market leaders.
	Whilst its central philosophy is one of zero pesticide and artificial fertiliser use, it is not considered by orthodox growers possible to totally satisfy market needs this way.

D. Protected Vegetables - Salads

Trends	At the retail point sales values are in excess of £750m. With concerted advertising in a changed food market, mushrooms have found acceptance in fast and prepared salad food. The growth of vegetarianism has also contributed to increased sales of salad vegetables.
	Oriental leafy brassicas (Pak Choi) and other stir-fry type vegetables are gaining favour with wok users for their flavour and simplicity.
Areas	Although the area has declined in the last decade, production techniques have doubled yield per hectare in tomatoes for example. The island of Guernsey has declined in importance to the UK, with Holland and Spain now major exporters to the British market.
	The high light areas of Britain - Sussex, Hampshire, Humberside and Lancashire, are the main growing areas. In addition to labour the next highest cost is fuel.
Technology	Energy saving techniques have been introduced (thermal screens) and gas, fuel oil and coals are used.
	The use of rockwool and nutrient film, plus sophisticated computer driven environmentally controlled glasshouses have revolutionised tomato, lettuce and cucumber growing.
Products	80% of the hectares of protected vegetables are salad crops (tomatoes, lettuce, cucumber, pepper). Mushrooms are a major commodity in this category, with an estimated turnover of £150m from 300 producers, of which three are the main suppliers.
Outlets	Large supply group co-operatives have been founded to meet the requirements of the supermarkets, who have a 60% market share of salads.
	An emerging sector of the salads industry is the protected leafy vegetables, which are mainly grown in plastic tunnels.

FLOWERS & BULBS

E. Field Grown Flowers and Bulbs

Trends
Early spring flower production in the mild areas of the South West continues to be an important enterprise. Bulb production has declined over recent years due to strong competition from the Dutch market.

Areas
Bulb production is predominant in Lincolnshire, the home of the major export, import and packing industries. Flower production is mainly in Cornwall and the Isles of Scilly.

Products
Narcissi and tulips are the main outdoor flower and bulb crops. Gladioli, roses, dahlias, chrysanthemums, irises and anemones have seen a resurgence of consumer demand recently.

Outlets
Bulbs are marketed dormant through garden centres, DIY stores and mail order. There is a significant export trade for bulbs. Flowers are marketed via wholesalers, direct retail outlets e.g. garden centres, some supermarkets, florists, van and roadside sales.

F. Protected Flowers

Cut Flowers

Trend
The impact of high energy costs, an economy in recession, and severe competition (from the Dutch Auction) has brought about changes in this sector, with reduced market share and declining hectares.

Compared to other European countries the UK has a very low per capita spend on flowers (£5.53 compared to Holland £38 and Germany £28 - Mintel 1989). However, flower expenditure had risen 85%, a trend which continues. The Plants and Flowers Association actively promotes pot plants and flowers.

Areas
The Channel Islands flower industry has maintained its presence in recent years, and added mail order flower sales to its services.

Products
Carnations, roses and chrysanthemums have been worst affected, the latter being the only survivor of note.

New crops like Alstroemerias have developed new market niches, as have specialist cut flowers for the floristry trade (e.g. Gypsophila).

Outlets
The value of cut flower sales is in excess of £650m at retail prices. 50% of sales are direct from the nursery or van sales, the rest from the wholesale market. Lingarden Ltd. and Grower Marketing Services Ltd. are two major flower selling co-operatives.

Bedding Plants

Trends
The quintessential feature of British bedding at home and in towns has created a marked growth in the past decade (8.9m in 1983 to over 22m in 1993).

Retail value of sales is estimated to be in excess of £125m in 1994.

POT PLANTS

Technology   Many growers have diversified into bedding to take up the demand, and taken advantage of improved cultural techniques and improved presentation.

"Colourpacks" have established themselves as a brand leader.

Products   Hanging baskets, patios, and autumn bedding have all created a new demand. Local authorities maintain bedding programmes central to their amenity plantings.

Outlets   Garden centres are the main sales outlet (80%). Potted plants for bedding currently run at 90m per year, against 11.3m in 1983.

Pot Plants

Trends   According to Mintel 1989 the retail value of sales reached £275m. The UK has a low per capita spend on pot plants, although at almost £5.00 in 1989 (Mintel) it has improved.

Areas   National hectarage has grown slightly (145 ha to 161 ha from 1988 to 1993). The Dutch remain the industry's major competitor, enjoying a large market share.

Technology   There are a small number of major suppliers targeting traditional demand periods (Easter, Christmas).

Products   Main flowering product lines are Azaleas, Pot Chrysanthemums, Cyclamen, Poinsettia and Saintpaulia, Ficus, Yucca, Hedera, and Chlorophytum are the main lines in the foliage sector.

Outlets   The supermarkets have an increased share of sales (Marks & Spencer plc with 12% dominate).

Traditional florists and greengrocers have 45% share. Garden centres, market stalls and roadside sellers share the rest.

G. Hardy Nursery Stock

Trends   In marketing terms this sector has been a major success in the past decade, representing today an estimated sales value of £1 billion annually. The emergence of the garden centre, and the development of containerised plants have contributed to an unprecedented demand.

Large DIY stores and multiples (Texas, B&Q, Sainsbury's Homebase) are an ever expanding sector.

Areas   Throughout the UK. The area of production is stable at about 7300 hectares, but there has been a substantial increase in container grown plants from 131m in 1979 to an estimated 350m in 1993.

Technology   Trees and plants, including roses, are still lifted in large numbers from open ground as 'bare-root' plants. Most of the 500 hardy plant nurseries are growing trees and shrubs, nearly 60% grow conifers, 27% herbaceous perennials and 20% alpines, 60% of all plant material is containerised.

HOPS

Products	In the tree section Prunus, Robinia, Birch and Acer remain leading lines, and in shrubs Potentilla, Berberis and Spiraea are favourites. Hosta, Lupin, Delphinium and Astilbe lead the herbaceous perennials, and Cupressus Leylandii, Hawthorn, Beech and Privet are the leading hedging and screening plants. Hedera and Clematis are the most popular climbers.

The health status and quality of material from propagation to sale has been radically improved in recent years. The increased interest in patios and hard standing areas has brought about the introduction of new plants. There has been a growth in ground cover plants and miniature roses.

Outlets	Gardening remains a major leisure industry for the private sector (it is estimated that there are 18.5m gardens in the UK), and the value placed on amenity plantings in the public (and private) sector is very high. Local authorities allocate large budgets to maintain and improve the environment of municipal parks, gardens and highways. It is estimated that there are about 100m amenity trees in suburban areas, occupying some 500,000 hectares of land (the same area as broad leaved forests in the UK). There is a 50:50 share of the hardy nursery stock market between the public and the private sectors.

Notes	A number of hardy nursery stock producers belong to co-operatives such as FARPLANTS in Sussex. The challenge to producers is to supply the large volume customers like local authorities and multiple stores.

H. Beverage Crops

Trends	British hop production has seen a slight increase in product quality, output value and export during the last few years, although the efficiency and ever-increasing economy in the use of hops has resulted in a steady diminution of demand generally. Vine growing for wine production has been depressed by recent EU regulations. Cider apple production remains important in the traditional orchard areas.

Areas	All crops are grown in the southern counties from Suffolk to the West Midlands, a mild climate and certain daylength being important criteria.

Products	Hops are sold either whole or as pellets or extract for processing by breweries. Grapes and cider apples are sometimes processed on the farm where a winery or cottage cider industry is attached. Elsewhere the fruit is transported to a manufacturer for processing.

Outlets	These are generally well-established industries, the crop being grown specifically for a processor or manufacturer e.g. Bulmers.

GRADING AND QUALITY STANDARDS

Just about all types of horticultural products are subject to grading standards of some sort. These may be set by the European Union, or for nursery stock - 'local' British H.T.A. Standards. Minimum standards are laid down for both edible and non edible produce.

Grading, fortunately, follows a standard format, although the actual specification will obviously vary across crop types.

Commodities Subject to Quality Standards

Edibles:

Fruit	Vegetables	Salads
Apples	Artichokes	Aubergines
Apricots	Asparagus	Chicory
Cherries	Beans (other than shelling)	Cucumbers
Grapes	Brussels Sprouts	Lettuce, Endives & Batavia
Kiwi	Cabbage	Sweet Peppers
Lemons	Carrots	Tomatoes
Mandarins	Cauliflowers	
Oranges	Celery	
Peaches	Courgettes	
Nectarines	Garlic	
Pears	Leeks	
Plums	Onions	
Strawberries	Peas	
	Spinach	

Source: E.C. Quality Standards for Horticultural Produce - MAFF.

Non Edibles:
Flowering bulbs, corms & tubers, cut flowers & foliage

QUALITY STANDARD

Quality Standard Layout

The general quality classification has the following Quality Standard Layout:

Quality Class	Description
Extra Class	Excellent quality & usually only very specially selected and presented produce.
Class I	Good quality produce with no defects.
Class II	Reasonably good quality, sound but deficient in 1 or 2 requirements such as shape, colour, smell, blemishes and marks.
Class III	Produce of marketable quality which is not up to the standard of higher class.
NB:	*Class III will only operate in special circumstances - e.g. shortage of supply - in recent years these have only been introduced for a limited period for witloof chicory & asparagus.*

You will find individual specifications under the appropriate crop type in the following Specialist Crop Sectors.

SPECIALIST SECTORS

A: SOFT FRUIT

NOTES

STRABERRIES

SECTION A: SOFT FRUIT

Introduction

This section looks at the main soft fruit enterprises: strawberries, raspberries, blackcurrants and gooseberries. Quality standards are only published for strawberries.

STRAWBERRIES

These are versatile plants being cultivated from the Equator almost to the Arctic Circle. In Europe the main crop is outdoor grown. They are also produced in glass houses, high and low plastic tunnels which produce fruit marketed for much of the year but because of high fuel costs, very out of season fruit is a luxury.

For growers, strawberries are a high risk crop. Not only do they face foreign competition but they have to match high quality standards particularly those required by multiples. The UK has a 5 month home produced strawberry season, although recent developments in new technology could mean that English strawberries will be available for at least seven months of the year. The main outdoor growing season is from late May extending through to October.

Availability from UK Producers

Jan	Feb	Mar	Apr	May	Jun	Jul	Aug	Sept	Oct	Nov	Dec
					▒	▒	▒	▒	▒		

Availability from Overseas Producers

	Jan	Feb	Mar	Apr	May	Jun	Jul	Aug	Sept	Oct	Nov	Dec
Spain	▒	▒	▒	▒	▒							
USA	▒		▒	▒	▒	▒	▒	▒	▒	▒	▒	
Netherlands			▒	▒	▒	▒	▒	▒	▒	▒		
Belgium / Lux.			▒	▒	▒	▒	▒	▒	▒	▒		

Key facts

Area Grown (ha)	5,605
Gross Production ('000t)	52
UK Market Size ('000t)	62.57
UK Market Share (%)	65.2
UK Exports ('000t)	0.38
UK Imports ('000t)	21.75

STRAWBERRIES

Grading Standards

	Extra	I	II	III
Normal	25 mm	22 mm		15 mm
Primella & Gariguette		18 mm		

No minimum sizes are laid down for wood strawberries.

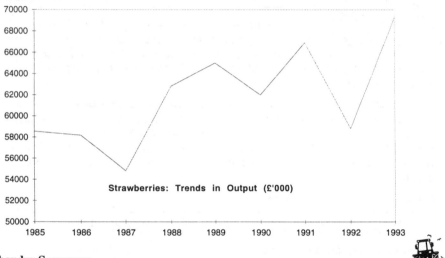

Strawberries: Trends in Output (£'000)

Husbandry Summary

Varieties   Elsanta is the leading June bearing variety. Honeoye is early, Symphony late. autumn fruiting varieties: Rapella, Evita, Tango

Sites & soils   Grade 1 soils are preferred on south facing slopes, although a range of site spreads production and harvesting. Free air drainage minimises frost damage and fungal attacks. Raised bed culture improves yield.

Environment Strawberries can be grown under glass, plastic tunnels, covered with cloches or layflat sheets (fleece, polythene). Windbreaks improve microclimate. Soil sterilisation may be necessary (Methyl bromide) against soil borne diseases.

Planting   30-40,000 plants/ha on two row, raised beds, often covered with black (or white) plastic. Multi-crowned runners can be planted through the plastic in May, to harvest in July, and for a second crop the following year. Alternatively crops can be grown on flat ground in single rows 90 cm x 37.5 cm, planting cold stored runners from March-August. The first crop is the following June. 2-3 crops are taken before quality declines.

autumn fruit varieties are generally pot grown under protection and planted out in April, to crop from July-October. One crop is taken, prices are generally higher.

Nutrition

Well manured soils are recommended with preplanting dressing of FYM (70t/ha). Pre-planting soil analysis is essential. Indices as for tree fruits. Foliar analysis and fertigation via the irrigation system will optimise plant requirements. High phosphates are required for plant establishment, and high potash to support high yields.

	Index 0 kg/ha	Index 3 kg/ha
Phosphate	75	12
Potash	250	33
Magnesium	62	33

Irrigation

It is not recommended to grow strawberries without irrigation. T-tapes are preferred for optimum effectiveness. Applications should match SMD's (soil moisture deficits) from April-July for main crop and April - September for ever bearers. Usual water requirements are 80-100 mm using conventional applicators, 60-80 mm through bed tapes. Yield gains of Class 1 fruit are 30-50%.

Production Cycle

Apr - Sept

Fallow new site, applying herbicides (Glyphosate) to eliminate perennial weeds. Subsoil, deep plough, cultivate, apply base fertiliser dressings. Prepare beds and install T-tape irrigation system. Sterilise soil against soil borne diseases (Verticillium Wilt, Red Core). Lay black plastic bed covers.

Feb

After coldest temperatures cover established crops with floating mulches/deep straw to manipulate earliness/lateness.

Mar

Plant orthodox cold stored runners, de-blossom, de-runner for next season.

Mar - Jun

Crop spray programme to control Aphid and Red Spider Mite, Mildew and Botrytis - the major pests and diseases. Biological control, using Phytoseilus, is effective for Mite control. Vine Weevil is a serious pest.

Apr

Plant potted everbearers. Irrigate to establish. Remove 1st flower flush.

Apr - May

(June for everbearers). Straw down to protect developing fruits.

May

Plant 60 day Elsanta. Irrigate, straw down as fruit trusses develop. In all cases only plant certified stock plants.

May - Jul

(July - Sept for everbearers). Maintain low SMD's with regular irrigation applications of 10-20 mm/week.

RASPBERRIES

May - Jul	(Aug - Oct for everbearers). Harvest main crop, mostly into 220 gm punnets. Very labour intensive (15 pickers/ha plus supervision and carting). In peak week x 2 required. Transfer to rapid cooling facility to achieve 5-8° C, prior to 'coolchain' marketing. Pick and pack daily.
Jul	Post harvest lightly mow off foliage, tidy up crop, including runner removal. Maintain low SMD's for full flower initiation.

RASPBERRIES

Raspberries used to come from Scotland, but now a majority of Scottish raspberries are frozen either Individual Fruit Quick Frozen (IQF) or as a block. Block frozen and commercially-preserved fruit are used for jam manufacturing. The main Scottish areas for growth are Ayr, Perth and Kinross.

Most of the English crop is sold fresh. However some freezing (IQF) takes place, mostly in Norfolk. The principal producing areas of England are Kent, Hereford, Worcester and Norfolk. Raspberries are grown to a lesser extent in Wales where they are cultivated for PYO and fresh farm sales.

Raspberries are mostly grown outdoors. Many summer fruiting varieties are bi-annual so both the existing fruiting canes and the young canes that will fruit in the following season are present in the same crop row during summer and autumn.

There has been a big increase in the area devoted to raspberry production in England and Wales in the last 10 years. This has resulted from the growth of Pick Your Own (PYO) outlets. Approximately 65% of the crop for fresh consumption and home preservation is now being grown for sale direct to the public by PYO.

The problem with commercial production is the difficulty in finding pickers when fruit is ready for marketing. This applies to all soft fruit.

In addition to the upsurge of interest in raspberries for sale via PYO, recent years have also seen increased sales through traditional outlets e.g. greengrocers and especially supermarkets. Raspberries perish very quickly and are usually frozen or used for jam making.

Availability from UK Producers

Jan	Feb	Mar	Apr	May	Jun	Jul	Aug	Sept	Oct	Nov	Dec
					▓	▓	▓	▓	▓		

Availability from Overseas Producers

	Jan	Feb	Mar	Apr	May	Jun	Jul	Aug	Sept	Oct	Nov	Dec
France						▓	▓	▓	▓	▓		
Chile	▓	▓	▓									
USA						▓	▓	▓	▓	▓		

RASPBERRIES

Area Grown (ha)	2,500
Gross Production ('000t)	19.3
UK Market Size ('000t)	18.58
UK Market Share (%)	96.3
UK Exports ('000t)	0.002
UK Imports ('000t)	0.70

Raspberries: Trends in Output (£'000)

Husbandry Summary

Varieties	Malling Leo, Malling Jewel, Glen Clova, Glen Moy and Glen Prosen. Primo cane varieties: autumn Bliss.
Soils	Grade 1 freely drained medium loams with water holding capacity preferred. A sheltered, frost free site is desirable.
Environment	Peripheral windbreaks improve microclimate, and reduce lateral damage. Internal windbreaks (Alder) dividing fields into 1-2 ha paddocks are beneficial. French tunnels (walk-in, plastic) are used for early production.
Planting	Cane rows are planted approx. 2.5m apart, and depending on variety, planted at 0.6m apart in the row. Plant population 6,667-7,000/ha. Certified material should be used. A post and wire support system needs to be

RASPBERRIES

erected in the 1st season of growth. 2 m round chestnut stakes, 6-8m apart in the row, will support 2 x 12 gauge wires at 0.5m and 1.2m. End and middle braces should be used to take crop load. Raspberry planting will last 10-12 years, 2 years to establish, 10 years cropping.

Nutrition   Well manured soils are recommended with preplanting dressing of FYM (70t/ha). Preplanting soil analysis is essential. Indices as for strawberries. Foliar spray (Urea for N, Magnesium, sulphate for Mg) very beneficial. Top dress annually with 100kg N, 150kg P and 200kg K per hectare.

Irrigation   Raspberries are very responsive to irrigation. Surface laid emitters or T-tape to maintain minimum SMD's of 5-10mm increase yield by 35-40%. Applications should be delayed until white fruit stage. Heavy straw mulches are beneficial.

Production Cycle

Apr - Sept   Fallow new site, applying herbicides (Glyphosate) to eliminate perennial weeds. Subsoil, deep plough, cultivate, apply base fertiliser dressings. Set out field with cane markers for plant rows.

Oct - Dec   Plant freshly lifted young canes from certified stock. Prune back to ground level in spring to stimulate basal growth. 2 - 4 new cane growths will emerge.

Mar +   Erect post and wirework.

Jun - Sept   Tie in new cane growth. Irrigate to optimise growth. Leave to harvest small tonnage in first year.

Sept - Dec   Following year. Prune out all old canes to ground level. Tie in new young cane growth, and lace onto top wire having secured the canes to the bottom wire. Mow off or desiccate surplus new cane growth. 5-8 healthy canes per stool to be tied in. Full cane population/metre run of wire is critical for optimum yield.

Feb - Mar   Apply annual residual herbicide (Bromacil). Spot treat perennials.

Mar - Jul   Apply crop protection programme. Aphid, Tortrix Caterpillar and Red Spider Mite are the main pests. Predatory mites are widely used. Raspberry Beetle and Cane Midge require carefully timed sprays. Apply approved fungicides to control Botrytis, Mildew and Cane Spot.

Jun - Oct   Varieties can extend the picking season. Carrying frames or picking trays are used to keep the punnets close to the crop. Colour specification is critical at harvest. 20-30 pickers/ha required. Daily or every other day picking essential. Rapid cooling of fruit extends shelf life. 'Coolchain' distribution assists marketing.

OUTSIDER'S GUIDE

BLACKCURRANTS

Along with the red and white varieties, blackcurrants cultivated in the UK today are derived from species native to Scandinavia, Siberia, North America, Northern Europe and North Africa. They were first seen in gardens in this country in the early 16th century. Today, blackcurrants are grown mainly in the West Midlands, Norfolk and Kent.

The breeding programme at the Scottish Crop Research Institute has produced a range of new varieties of blackcurrant which have enjoyed popularity with growers and processors. These varieties include Ben Lomond, introduced in the mid-1970's and Ben Alder, available from 1988.

These and other varieties such as Ben Sarak and Ben More are more resistant to frost. Ben Lomond, which has berries significantly larger than many other varieties, is a blackcurrant that makes excellent jam and is also appreciated for juice processing. PYO is now an important outlet for sales of fresh blackcurrants.

Availability from UK Producers

Jan	Feb	Mar	Apr	May	Jun	Jul	Aug	Sept	Oct	Nov	Dec
						░░░	░░░				

Availability from Overseas Producers

	Jan	Feb	Mar	Apr	May	Jun	Jul	Aug	Sept	Oct	Nov	Dec
France							░░░	░░░				

Key Facts

Area Grown (ha)	3,466
Gross Production ('000t)	29.9
UK Market Size ('000t)	26.02
UK Market Share (%)	96.6
UK Exports ('000t)	0.47
UK Imports ('000t)	0.90

BLACKCURRANTS

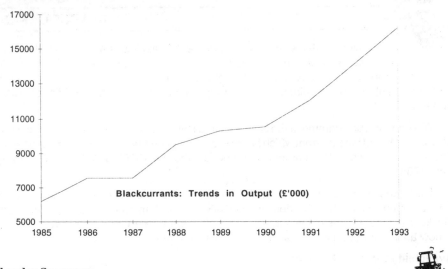

Blackcurrants: Trends in Output (£'000)

Husbandry Summary

Varieties	Baldwin, Ben Lomond, Ben Sarak, Ben More
Sites & soils	A sheltered, frost free, south facing site is preferred. Well drained medium loam soils are best.
Environment	Peripheral windbreaks improve microclimate. Wind damage can be severe. Internal windbreaks (Alder) dividing fields into 1-2 ha paddocks are beneficial.
Planting	Rectangular plant 2.7m x 0.6 m giving a plant population of 6,172 bushes/ha. 1 year old certified material is used, planted in single rows. The life of a blackcurrant plantation is 10-15 years. Establishment can be done by hardwood cuttings, planted through black plastic strips. If machine picked, minimum of 12-15ha should be established.
Nutrition	Well manured soils are recommended with preplanting dressing of FYM (70t/ha). Preplanting soil analysis is essential. Indices as for strawberries. Base dress with 160khg N, 60kg P, 100kg K per hectare. Top dress annually with 700kg N, 50kg P and 70kg K per hectare.
Irrigation	Blackcurrants are responsive to irrigation. Surface laid emitters or T-tape to maintain minimum SMD's of 5-10mm increase yield by 25-35%. Solid set sprinklers are used for frost protection/irrigation. Good soil drainage is essential. Access to larger volumes of water required. For yield gain, applications should be delayed until early fruit development stage. Heavy straw mulches are beneficial.

Apr - Sept	Fallow new site, applying herbicides (Glyphosate) to eliminate perennial weeds. Subsoil, deep plough, cultivate, apply base fertiliser dressings. Set out field with cane markers for plant rows.
Oct - Dec	Plant freshly lifted young 1 yr. bushes from certified stock. Cut down to ground level after planting. Apply residual herbicides (Simazine) post planting.
Mar	Apply straw mulch. Rogue bushes for Big Bud and burn.
Jun - Sept	Irrigate to optimise growth in first summer. Spot treat perennial weeds.
Mar - Jul	Apply crop protection programme: Aphid, Gall Mite, Leaf Midge, Caterpillar and Capsid are the main pests. Blackcurrant Gall Mite is a serious pest, carrying the reversion virus. Gall mites cause 'Big Bud' of blackcurrants. Apply approved fungicides to control Leaf Spot, American Gooseberry Mildew and Botrytis. Routine 7-10 day prophylactic sprays are recommended.
Jul - Aug	Varieties will extend the picking season. Hand harvesting necessary in first two years. Thereafter machine pick.
Aug - Sept	Apply post harvest herbicides (MCPA) for broad-leaved weeds.

GOOSEBERRIES

GOOSEBERRIES

Gooseberries are native to Europe and North Africa. The main dessert variety is called Leveller. Principal growing areas are Kent, Worcestershire, Isle of Ely, West Norfolk, South Holland (Lincolnshire), Hampshire, Lancashire, Cornwall. Gooseberries are cultivated outdoors on bushes which need to be planted on distinct legs or stems.

Over recent years much work has been carried out as part of a programme at the Institute of Horticultural Research to incorporate disease resistance into commercially attractive varieties.

Availability from UK Producers

Jan	Feb	Mar	Apr	May	Jun	Jul	Aug	Sept	Oct	Nov	Dec
					░░░	░░░	░░░				

Availability from Overseas Producers

	Jan	Feb	Mar	Apr	May	Jun	Jul	Aug	Sept	Oct	Nov	Dec
Hungary						░░░						
Poland						░░░						

Key Facts

Area Grown (ha)	**1,150**
Gross Production ('000t)	**n/a**
UK Market Size ('000t)	**0.40**
UK Market Share (%)	**n/a**
UK Exports ('000t)	**n/a**
UK Imports ('000t)	**0.40**

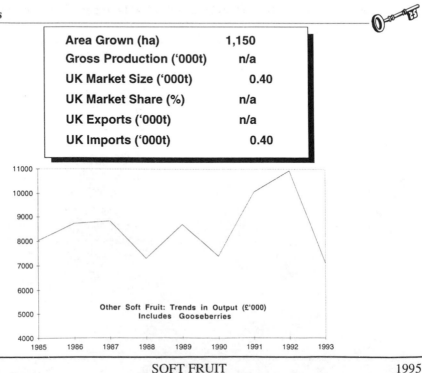

Other Soft Fruit: Trends in Output (£'000)
Includes Gooseberries

GOOSEBERRIES

Husbandry Summary

Varieties	Careless, Invicta (Jubilee Clone), Keepsake, May Duke, Whinam's Industry, Greenfinch.
Soils	Gooseberries grow on a wide range of soils. Good drainage is essential.
Environment	Peripheral windbreaks improve microclimate. Internal windbreaks (Alder) dividing fields into 1-2ha paddocks are beneficial.
Planting	Rectangular plant 2.5m x 0.9m giving a plant population of 4,444 bushes/ha. 2 year old certified material is used, planted in single rows. Multirow, bed systems have been grown successfully, achieving higher plant populations and increased yields. The life of a gooseberry plantation is 15-20 years.
Nutrition	Well manured soils are recommended with preplanting dressing of FYM (70t/ha). Preplanting soil analysis is essential. Indices as for strawberries. Base dress with 150kg N, 150kg P, 225kg K per hectare. Top dress annually with 50kg N, 50kg P, 75kg K per hectare.
Irrigation	Gooseberries are responsive to irrigation. Surface laid emitters or T-tape to maintain minimum SMD's of 5-10mm increase yield by 35-40%. Application should be delayed until early fruit stage. Heavy straw mulches are beneficial.

Production Cycle

Apr - Sept	Fallow new site, applying herbicides (Glyphosate) to eliminate perennial weeds. Subsoil, deep plough, cultivate, apply base fertiliser dressings. Set out field with cane markers for plant rows.
Oct - Dec	Plant freshly lifted young 2yr bushes from certified stock. Tip laterals to build 4-5 frame branches. Apply residual herbicides.
March +	Apply straw mulch.
Jun - Sept	Irrigate to optimise growth. Spot treat perennial weeds.
Mar - Jul	Apply crop protection programme: Aphid, Sawfly Caterpillar and Capsid are the main pests. Predatory mites are widely used. Apply approved fungicides to control American Gooseberry Mildew, Leaf Spot and Botrytis.
Apr - May	Hand thin if heavy cropset.
Jun - Oct	Varieties can extend the picking season. Carrying frames are used to keep the market trays close to the crop. Processors will provide own trays.

SUMMARY

SOFT FRUIT FINANCIAL INFORMATION

Enterprise Item	Strawberries	Raspberries	Blackcurrants	Gooseberries
Production & Marketing				
Percentage in a mixed fruit farm	-	-	-	-
Total UK hectares	5,605	2,500	3,466	1,150
Estimated producer numbers	2,000	1,500	500	n/a
Average unit size (ha)	4 - 6	4 - 6	6 - 10	1 - 3
Average yeld (t/ha)	8 - 12	4 - 6	5	5
Marketing Channels	Grower co-ops, Kentish Garden, PYO, wholesale markets, processors		Processors (Beechams) wholesalers, PYO, multiples	PYO, wholesalers. processors
Investment Considerations				
Typical investment/ha (£)	4 - 9 a	2.5	2 - 3	2.2 b
Minimum size of unit (ha)	2 - 5	2 - 5	15	2 - 5
Lead time to first crop (years)	1	2	1	2
Production cycles thereafter	1 - 2	10	10	15
Cycles per year	1	1	1	1
Rotational details	Red Core, Crown Rot, Verticillium Wilt (soil sterilisation recommended)	Some soil borne diseases	None	None

a   Excluding fast cooling/holding facilities & small packing facility.
b   Excluding machine harvester (costs £60,000 to £70,000). Alternative to buying is to
     use contractors which cost £2,500 to £4,000/ha.

Soft Fruit Gross Margins

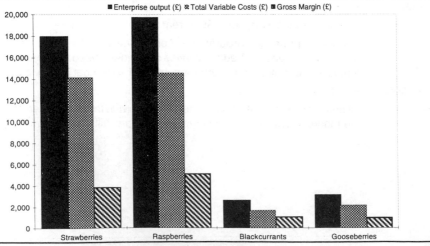

■ Enterprise output (£) ⊠ Total Variable Costs (£) ■ Gross Margin (£)

Enterprise Item	Strawberries	Raspberries	Blackcurrants	Gooseberries
Example variety	Elsanta & Others	Glen Clova Leo - various	Baldwin, Ben Lomond	Various including Leveller
OUTPUT				
Yield /ha (tonnes)	12 [a]	9	6	7
Price/tonne (£)	1,500	2,200	450	450
Enterprise output (£)	**18,000**	**19,800**	**2,700**	**3,150**
VARIABLE COSTS - Production				
Fertilisers	56	70	60	45
Sprays	595	620	380	105
Plants	2,960	250[b]	198 [c]	147 [d]
Straw	75	10	-	-
Water	250	250	100	-
Casual labour	4,560	7,920	-	875
Sub total	**8,496**	**9,120**	**738**	**1,172**
VARIABLE COSTS - Marketing				
Grading / packing (labour [e])	1,056	792	468 [f]	-
Packaging	2,160	2,250	-	378
Carriage / handling	624	450	-	294
Commission (10%)	1,852	1,980	-	315
Sub total	**5,692**	**5,472**	**468**	**987**
Total variable costs (£)	**14,188**	**14,592**	**1,206**	**2,159**
Gross margin (£/ha)	**3,812**	**5,208**	**1,494**	**991**

a   June bearing varieties only

b   £2,500 establishment costs written off over 10 years

c   £1,988 establishment costs written off over 10 years

d   £2,200 establishment costs written off over 15 years

e   Assumes % to supermarkets (cooling, weighing, labelling, lidding etc.) and % to wholesale market say 50:50.

f   Machine harvesting using contractors, including carriage/handling, casual harvesting labour with machine.

SUMMARY

SPECIALIST SECTORS

B: TOP FRUIT

NOTES

APPLES

SECTION B: TOP FRUIT

Introduction

This section looks at the main top fruit crops; these are dessert and culinary apples, pears, plums and cherries.

APPLES

There are approximately 1,022 registered commercial apple growers in the UK. Northern Ireland has a significant apple growing industry predominantly Bramley Seedling. English apples represent approximately 38% of the total 'country of origin' share of identified eating apples; France 34%, South Africa 16%, New Zealand 9%, Chile 2% and others 8%.

The 1995 EU 'Grubbing-up Grant' designed to encourage Mediterranean growers to get out of apple production, has had a detrimental effect on the British orchard hectarage. Prices have been low during the last ten years and British producers are taking up the considerable grants offered under the scheme, with the effect that 15% of England's apple orchards are to go under the bulldozer.

Many famous English apples are said to be better tasting when they are smaller in size. This applies to Cox's Orange Pippin, Egremont, Russet, Discovery, Spartan, Idared and Worcester Pearmain. In Britain we have a preference for red skinned and red flush apples rather than the green variety. Apples for juicing must be of good quality. Top fruit is susceptible to handling damage.

Availability from UK Producers

Jan	Feb	Mar	Apr	May	Jun	Jul	Aug	Sept	Oct	Nov	Dec
▓	▓	▓	▓	▓	▓		▓	▓	▓	▓	▓

Availability from Overseas Producers

	Jan	Feb	Mar	Apr	May	Jun	Jul	Aug	Sept	Oct	Nov	Dec
France	▓	▓						▓	▓	▓	▓	▓
South Africa	▓		▓	▓	▓	▓	▓	▓	▓		▓	▓
New Zealand			▓	▓	▓	▓	▓	▓	▓	▓	▓	▓
USA	▓	▓	▓	▓	▓	▓	▓	▓	▓	▓	▓	▓

APPLES

Key Facts:

	Dessert	Both	Culinary
Area Grown (ha)	12,400		7,700
Gross Production ('000t)	198.1		178.8
UK Market Size ('000t)		746	
UK Market Share (%)		38.6	
UK Exports ('000t)		37.8	
UK Imports ('000t)	458.4		Nil

Grading Standards

Apples	Extra	I	II	III
Large fruit	70 mm	65 mm	65 mm	50 mm
Other varieties	60 mm	55 mm	55 mm	50 mm

Also colouring criteria for each class - variety dependent.

Group A	Red varieties	
Group B	Mixed red colouring	Russetting and definition of large
Group C	Striped varieties	varieties also taken into consideration
Group D	Others	

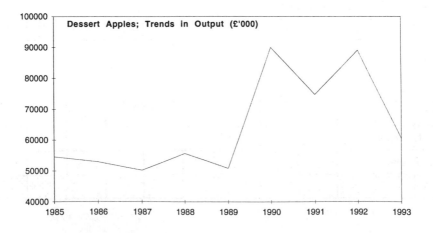

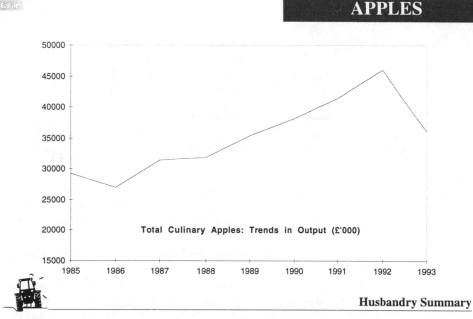

Total Culinary Apples: Trends in Output (£'000)

Husbandry Summary

Varieties	Dessert apples - Cox Orange Pippin (Queen Cox Clone), Gala, Discovery, Fiesta, Russet.
	Culinary apples - Bramley Seedling, Howgate Wonder, Lord Derby.
Rootstocks	Most common M27 very dwarfing, M9 dwarfing, M26 semi-dwarfing, MM106 vigorous. Tree populations/hectare from 2500 - 750 dependent on soil and system.
Systems	Very intensive 'super-spindles' will produce high early yields (within 3-5 years). 4 row bed systems are widely planted (3000/ha). Semi-intensive systems (on MM106) on poorer soils at 750/ha. Trend is higher investment, earlier break-even year, and shorter orchard life (12-15 years).
Environment	Gentle south facing slopes are preferred to drain cold air in spring (May frosts). Perimeter windbreaks should be planted (Poplar, Alder) to improve microclimate, and orchards 'paddocked' into 1-2 ha blocks with internal Alder windbreaks.
	2. A wide range of soils can be used, pH of 6-6.5 ideal. Free draining soils essential. Orchards should be protected from rabbits by a perimeter fence, or individual trees guarded. A grass sward is recommended. Irrigation is desirable.
Nutrition	Soil analysis for P, K, and Mg pre-planting and every 4-5 years. Nitrogen rarely needed unless soils poor.

APPLES

	Index 0 kg/ha	Index 3 kg/ha
Phosphate	75	12
Potash	250	33
Magnesium	62	33

Foliar sprays are widely used - Epsom Salts (Magnesium Sulphate) and Urea (Nitrogen) and Calcium Nitrate (Ca).

Production Cycle

Jun - Oct In year prior to planting: on fallowed site apply herbicides to perennial weeds (Glyphosate). Deep sub soil, plough, cultivate and sow over with grass. Stake up with 2.2m stakes and take out planting holes in October. Band spray tree rows.

Oct Apply P, K, Mg fertilisers, post harvest Urea foliar sprays, and autumn herbicides.

Nov - Mar Plant new orchard, and tie to stakes. Laterals tied down after planting to encourage fruit development. Minimal pruning as tree develops. Pyramidal shaped trees are widely grown, 1.25m wide and 2.5m tall in single rows or beds.

Apr - May Apply spring herbicides for annual/perennial weed control. Apply N and foliar sprays of N and Mg. Introduce beehives (1 hive per 2 ha) to assist pollination.

Mar - Sept 7-14 day routine prophylactic sprays should be applied. Caterpillar, Aphids, Red Spider Mite are controlled by various compounds. Scab and Mildew are the major diseases controlled by protectant fungicides. Predators (Typhlodromus) are used to biologically control red spider. Growth regulators (Cultar) are used.

May - Jun Apply fruit thinning agents (Carbaryl) and hand thin to establish the optimum number of fruitlets/tree. 65-70mm target size.

May - Sept Maintain soil moisture deficits within 25-50 mm using small droplet applicators, drip lines or rain guns.

Jul - Aug Remove excess growth by summer pruning to maintain fruit quality and improve fruit bud formation. Tie down new laterals for increased production.

Aug - Oct Harvest early varieties in sequence. Following fruit analysis in August (especially Ca) main varieties for storage will be harvested between 10 and 20 Sept (an optimum corridor). Fruit is picked into bulk bins (320kg) and transported to store. Quality control at harvest is essential. Pre-storage drenching of bins with fungicides minimises fruit rots in store. Anti-scald drenches are used for Bramley.

Sept-Apr (Cox)

PEARS

Aug - June (Bramley)

Store fruit at optimum regimes:

Variety	Duration	Temp°C	O_2 %	CO_2 %
Cox	Sept - Apr	3.5	1.25	0
Bramley	Aug - June	4.5	2.0	6

Inspect stores daily, and regularly sample. Store environments can be maintained automatically. When outloaded fruit should be graded by quality and size into trays, cells or loose.

PEARS

The UK crop is mainly grown in Kent & East Sussex and supplies 20% of the home market. Major imports are from France, Italy, Australia, New Zealand, South Africa, Spain and the Netherlands.

Pears can withstand less favourable soil types than apples.

The majority of pears grown in the UK are 'Conference'. There are hopes that a new variety will be available soon called Concorde which is a Conference/Comice cross and has good yield, texture, flavour and shape. Conference pears are dual purpose and can be cooked or eaten raw. (Pear growers also belong to English Apples & Pears Ltd.)

Availability from UK Producers

Jan	Feb	Mar	Apr	May	Jun	Jul	Aug	Sept	Oct	Nov	Dec
▒	▒	▒	▒	▒	▒			▒	▒	▒	▒

Availability from Overseas Producers

	Jan	Feb	Mar	Apr	May	Jun	Jul	Aug	Sept	Oct	Nov	Dec
South Africa		▒	▒	▒	▒	▒						
Netherlands	▒	▒	▒	▒				▒	▒	▒	▒	▒
France	▒	▒						▒	▒	▒	▒	▒
Italy	▒	▒	▒	▒					▒	▒		▒

PEARS

Area Grown (ha)	**3,600**
Gross Production ('000t)	**43.7**
UK Market Size ('000t)	**138.17**
UK Market Share (%)	**20.1**
UK Exports ('000t)	**2.69**
UK Imports ('000t)	**110.36**

Grading Standards

Also colouring criteria for each class - variety dependent (as apples).

Pears	Extra	I	II	III
Large varieties	60 mm	55 mm	55 mm	45 mm
Others	55 mm	50 mm	45 mm	45 mm

Group A	Red varieties	
Group B	Mixed Red Colouring	Russetting and definition of large
Group C	Striped varieties	varieties also taken into consideration
Group D	Others	

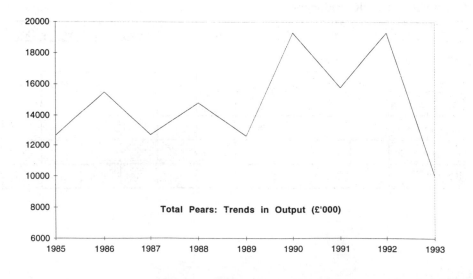

Total Pears: Trends in Output (£'000)

OUTSIDER'S GUIDE

Husbandry Summary

Varieties	Conference, Comice, Concorde, William's Bon Chretien
Rootstocks	Quince C and Quince A

Systems   Semi-intensive and intensive plantings are common 4.3m x 2.5m (930 trees/ha). Multi-row beds (3-4) have been planted (2500 trees/ha). Maiden or two year old certified trees should be planted. Trend is higher investment, earlier break-even year, and shorter orchard life (12-15 years).

Environment   Gentle south facing slopes are preferred to drain cold air in Spring (May frosts). Perimeter windbreaks should be planted (Poplar, Alder) to improve microclimate, and orchards paddocked into 1-2 ha blocks with internal Alder windbreaks.

A wide range of soils can be used, pH of 6-6.5 ideal. Free draining soils essential. Orchards should be protected from rabbits by a perimeter fence, or individual trees guarded. A grass sward is recommended. Irrigation is desirable. Bullfinches can be a serious problem if trees grown near woodland.

Nutrition   Soil analysis for P, K and Mg pre-planting. Repeat every 4-5 years.

	Index 0 kg/ha	Index 3 kg/ha
Phosphate	75	12
Potash	250	33
Magnesium	62	33

Annual dressings of 120kg N, 25kg P, 40kg K and 50kg Mg are recommended per hectare.

Production Cycle

Jun - Oct   In year prior to planting: on fallowed site apply herbicides to perennial weeds (Glyphosate). Deep sub-soil, plough, cultivate and sow over with grass. Stake up with 2.2m stakes and take out planting holes in October.

Oct   Apply P, K, Mg fertilisers, post harvest Urea foliar sprays and autumn herbicides.

Nov - Mar   Plant new orchard, and tie to stakes. Laterals tied down after planting to encourage fruit development. Light tipping to develop main laterals. Pyramidal shaped trees are widely grown.

Apr - May   Apply spring herbicides for annual/perennial weed control. Apply N and foliar sprays of N and Mg. Introduce beehives (1 per 2ha) to assist pollination.

PLUMS

Mar - Sept	7-14 day routine prophylactic sprays should be applied. Caterpillar, Aphid, Red Spider Mite, Pear Midge and Leaf Blister Mite are controlled by various compounds. Scab is the major disease controlled by protectant fungicides. Predators (Typhlodromus) are used to biologically control red spider. Growth regulators (Cultar) are used.
May - Jun	Following a good set hand thinning may be necessary. This should be delayed until 'crook' stage.
May - Sept	Maintain soil moisture deficits within 25-50 mm using small droplet applicators, drip lines or rain guns.
Jul - Aug	Remove excess growth by summer pruning to improve fruit bud formation. Tie down new laterals for increased production.
Aug - Oct	Harvest early varieties in sequence. Main varieties for storage will be picked between Sept. 5-14 (an optimum corridor). Fruit is picked into bulk bins (320kg) and transported to store.
	Quality control at harvest is essential. Pre-storage drenching of bins with fungicides minimises fruit rots in store.
Sept - April	Store fruit at optimum regimes Conference 0.5-1°C, 5% oxygen, 5% carbon dioxide. Store reading should be taken daily, and regularly sample. Store environments can be maintained automatically. When outloaded fruit should be graded by quality and size into trays, cells or loose.

PLUMS

Most home grown plums are cultivated in Kent, the West Midlands and Eastern Counties. We import from France, Italy, South Africa and Chile.

The traditional sales outlet for plums has been for processing. This market has declined rapidly in the last few years as has the area of plums grown for the domestic market. The future of the industry lies in the establishment of new intensive orchards that are carefully managed to provide a large top quality fruit.

The Victoria variety is self fertile and needs no other variety to provide cross-pollination. Others are self sterile and will only produce a good crop when planted with other compatible varieties which flower at the same time.

Availability from UK Producers

Jan	Feb	Mar	Apr	May	Jun	Jul	Aug	Sept	Oct	Nov	Dec

Availability from Overseas Producers

	Jan	Feb	Mar	Apr	May	Jun	Jul	Aug	Sept	Oct	Nov	Dec
Spain					▒	▒	▒	▒	▒			
USA					▒	▒	▒	▒	▒	▒	▒	

Key Facts

Area Grown (ha)	2,300
Gross Production ('000t)	31.70
UK Market Size ('000t)	55.87
UK Market Share (%)	39.9
UK Exports ('000t)	0.50
UK Imports ('000t)	33.57

Grading Standards

Three classes : Extra, Class I and Class II

	Extra & I	II
Large fruit varieties	35 mm	30 mm
Other varieties	28 mm	25 mm
Mirabelles, Damsons & Plums of Rio	20 mm	17 mm

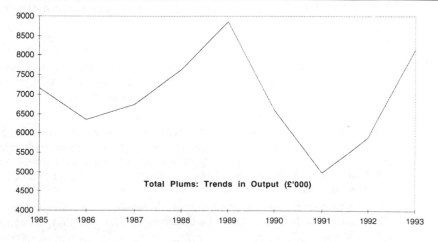

Total Plums: Trends in Output (£'000)

PLUMS

Husbandry Summary

Varieties	Victoria, Opal, Avalon, Excalibur, Cambridge Gage, Warwickshire Drooper, Czar.
Rootsocks	St Julian A, Pixy.
Systems	Semi intensive and intensive plantings are common 4.3m x 2.5m (930 trees/ha). Multi-row beds (3 rows) have been planted (2500 trees/ha). Maiden or two year old certified trees should be planted. Summer pruned, semi-dwarf pyramids are widely planted. Pruning plum trees in the winter should be avoided to minimise risk of silver leaf infection.
Environment	Gentle south facing slopes are preferred to drain cold air in spring (April frosts). Perimeter windbreaks should be planted (Poplar, Alder) to improve microclimate, and orchards paddocked into 1-2 ha. blocks with internal Alder windbreaks.
	A wide range of soils can be used, pH of 6-6.5 ideal. Free draining soils essential. Orchards should be protected from rabbits by a perimeter fence, or individual trees guarded. A grass sward is recommended. Irrigation is desirable.
Nutrition	Soil analysis for P, K and Mg pre-planting. Repeat every 4 - 5 years.

	Index 0 kg/ha	Index 3 kg/ha
Phosphate	75	12
Potash	250	33
Magnesium	62	33

Annual dressings of 150kg N, 40kg P, 80kg K, and 50kg Mg are recommended per hectare.

Production Cycle

Jun - Oct	In year prior to planting: on fallowed site apply herbicides to perennial weeds (Glyphosate). Deep sub-soil, plough, cultivate and sow over with grass. Stake up with 2.2m stakes and take out planting holes in October.
Oct	Apply N, P, K Mg fertilisers.
Nov - Mar	Plant new orchard, and tie to stakes. Laterals tied down after planting to encourage fruit development. Light tipping to develop main laterals. Pyramidal shaped trees are widely grown. Any pruning cuts painted against silver leaf infection. Tar oil winter washes applied. Protect trees with cotton thread (or Scaraweb) if attacked by bullfinches.
Apr	Apply spring herbicides for annual/perennial weed control. Apply N and foliar sprays of N, Mg. Introduce beehives (1 hive per 2ha) to assist pollination.

CHERRIES

Mar - Sept	At specific growth stages sprays should be applied. Caterpillar, Aphid, Red Spider Mite, Mealy Plum Aphid, Plum Rust, Rust Mite are controlled by various compounds. Bacterial canker sprays should be applied at leaf fall. Predators (Typhlodromus) are used to biologically control red spider. Plums are responsive to growth regulators (Cultar).
Jun	Following a good set hand thinning may be necessary to space fruitlets every 4-6 mm along branches.
May - Sept	Maintain soil moisture deficits within 25-50 mm using small droplet applicators, drip lines or rain guns.
Jul - Aug	Remove excess growth by summer pruning to improve fruit bud formation and maintain pyramidal tree shaper. Vigorous upright wood removed.
Aug - Oct	Harvest early varieties in sequence. Quality control at harvest is essential. Size and quality grading in field or packhouse is recommended. 5kg trays are widely used.

CHERRIES

Cherries were first introduced into Britain during the 1st Century by the Romans, who discovered sweet varieties growing wild in Western Asia. Sour types are thought to have originated from Eastern Europe and around the Caspian Sea. As a result of careful cultivation and experimentation over the years there are many varieties of cherry, but commercially only a limited number are grown.

Modern cherry orchards use a less vigorous rootstock producing smaller trees which can be planted closer together, are easier to harvest without the need for long ladders, bear fruit earlier in the tree's life and can be protected from bird damage - a major problem - by netting the entire orchard. British cherry growing has been through a difficult period, most recently during the Great Storm of October 1987 when orchards in the South East, the main production area, were totally destroyed. Replanting is being continued to restore and improve production.

Availability from UK Producers

Jan	Feb	Mar	Apr	May	Jun	Jul	Aug	Sept	Oct	Nov	Dec
					▓	▓	▓				

Availability from Overseas Producers

	Jan	Feb	Mar	Apr	May	Jun	Jul	Aug	Sept	Oct	Nov	Dec
USA						▓	▓	▓				
France				▓	▓	▓						
Italy					▓	▓						
Turkey				▓	▓	▓						

CHERRIES

Key Facts

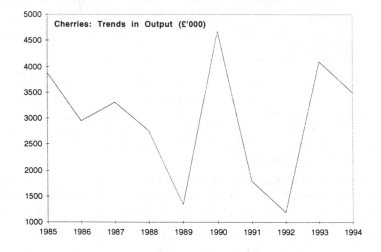

Area Grown (ha)	870
Gross Production ('000t)	4.2
UK Market Size ('000t)	13.09
UK Market Share (%)	29.8
UK Exports ('000t)	0.30
UK Imports ('000t)	9.19

Cherries: Trends in Output (£'000)

Granding Standards

Not available

Husbandry Summary

Varieties   Dessert: Stella, Van, Lapins, Colney, Mermat, Merchant, Merton Glory, Sunburst.

Culinary: Morello.

Rootstocks   Colt

Systems   Semi-intensive and intensive plantings are common 5.5m x 3.5m (520 trees/ha). Multi-row beds (3-4 rows) have been planted (2500 trees/ha). Maiden or two year old certified trees should be planted. Pruning cherry trees in the winter should be avoided to minimise risk of bacterial canker and silver leaf infection.

CHERRIES

Environment Gentle south facing slopes are preferred to drain cold air in spring (April frosts). Perimeter windbreaks should be planted (Poplar, Alder) to improve microclimate, and orchards 'paddocked' into 1-2 ha blocks with internal Alder windbreaks.

A wide range of soils can be used, pH 6-6.5 ideal. Free draining soils essential. Orchards should be protected from rabbits by a perimeter fence, or individual trees guarded. A grass sward is recommended. Irrigation is desirable.

Post and wirework to support a full field netting system may be necessary to protect trees from bird damage at harvest. Summer rainfall, causing fruit splitting, can cause very high crop losses at harvest. Newer varieties are less susceptible.

Nutrition Soil analysis for P, K and Mg pre-planting. Repeat every 4-5 years.

	Index 0 kg/ha	Index 3 kg/ha
Phosphate	75	12
Potash	250	33
Magnesium	62	33

Annual dressings of 40kg N, 20kg P, 40kg K are recommended per hectare.

Production Cycle

Jun - Oct In year prior to planting: on fallowed site apply herbicides to perennial weeds (Glyphosate). Deep sub-soil, plough, cultivate and sow over with grass. Stake up with 1.6m stakes and take out planting holes in October.

Oct Apply N, P, K, Mg fertilisers.

Nov - Mar Plant new orchard, and tie to stakes. Laterals tied down after plating to encourage fruit development. Light tipping to develop main laterals. Any pruning cuts painted against silver leaf infection. Tar oil winter washes applied. Protect trees with cotton thread (or Scaraweb) if attacked by bullfinches.

Apr Apply spring herbicides for annual/perennial weed control. Apply N and foliar sprays of N, Mg. Introduce beehives (1 hive per 2 ha) to assist pollination.

Mar - Sept At specific growth stages sprays should be applied. Caterpillar, Aphid, Red Spider Mite are controlled by various compounds. Bacterial canker sprays should be applied at leaf fall (mid August to mid Oct) and again at bud burst. Cherries are responsive to growth regulators (Cultar) producing more compact trees for easier and quicker harvesting.

May - Sept Maintain soil moisture deficits within 25-50 mm using small droplet applicators or drip lines.

SUMMARY

Jul - Aug   After harvest remove excess growth by summer pruning to improve fruit bud formation. Vigorous upright wood removed.

Harvest varieties in sequence. Protect crop from devastation by birds. Quality control at harvest is essential. 5 kg trays are widely used.

TOP FRUIT: FINANCIAL INFORMATION

Enterprise Item	Dessert Apples	Culinary Apples	Pears	Plums	Cherries
Production & Marketing					
Percentage in a mixed fruit farm	80%	10%	10%	10 - 30%	5 - 10%
Total UK hectares	12400	7700	3600	2300	870
Estimated producer numbers	1000	800	800	300	300
Average unit size (ha)	12 - 15	12 - 15	12 - 15	12 - 15	12 - 15
Average yield (t/ha)	16 - 30	20 - 40	7 - 10	8 - 12	3 - 4
Marketing channels	ENFRU Ltd. Orchard World Ltd .Other grower co-ops, whole sales markets & farm shops	As dessert apples with merchants processors, cider and juice makers		as dessert plus processors , Vale Plums	Grower Co-ops (HGF Kentish Gardens)
Investment Considerations					
Typical investment/ha (£) [a]	5,000 - 15,000	5,000 - 15,000	5,000 - 15,000	5,000 - 10,000	5,000 - 10,000 [b]
Minimum size of unit (ha)	10	10	10	10	5
Lead time to first crop (years)	2 - 3	3 - 4	5 - 6	2 - 3	2 - 3
Production cycles thereafter	10-15	15	15 - 20	15	15
Cycles per year	1	1	1	1	1
Rotational details	Specific apple replant disease (SARD) sterilisation may be needed	None	None	None	

a   Depending upon tree density/hectare. Also for apples and pears investment in storage, grading and packing facilities is not recommended. Membership of existing co-operatives and/or hire facilities recommended. Annual costs included in variable costs of marketing.

b   Cherries: excludes netting for bird protection.

SUMMARY

Top Fruit: Gross Margins

Enterprise Item	Dessert Apples	Culinary Apples	Pears	Plums	Cherries
Example variety	Cox Orange Pippin	Bramley	Conference	Victoria	Various
OUTPUT					
Yield /ha (tonnes)	24	32	15	15	8
Price/tonne (£)	400	250	400	560	1,000
Enterprise output (£)	**9,600**	**8,000**	**6,000**	**8,400**	**8,000**
VARIABLE COSTS - Production					
	£	£	£	£	£
Ferts	60	80	50	75	50
Sprays	425	490	260	135	89
Levies / advice	60	60	60	30	30
Sundries	75	50	75	35	85
Casual labour	650	700	525	1,650	2,000
Sub total Production (£)	**1,270**	**1,380**	**970**	**1,925**	**2,254**
VARIABLE COSTS - Marketing					
Grading / packing	768	1024	580	-	-
Packaging	1,008	1,344	765	1,072	560
Carriage / handling	912	1216	615	761	400
Commission (10%)	960	800	600	840	800
Sub total marketing (£)	**3,648**	**4,384**	**2,860**	**2,673**	**1,760**
Total variable Costs (£)	**4,918**	**5,764**	**3,530**	**4,598**	**4,014**
Gross margin (£)	**4,682**	**2,236**	**2,470**	**3,802**	**3,986**

NOTES

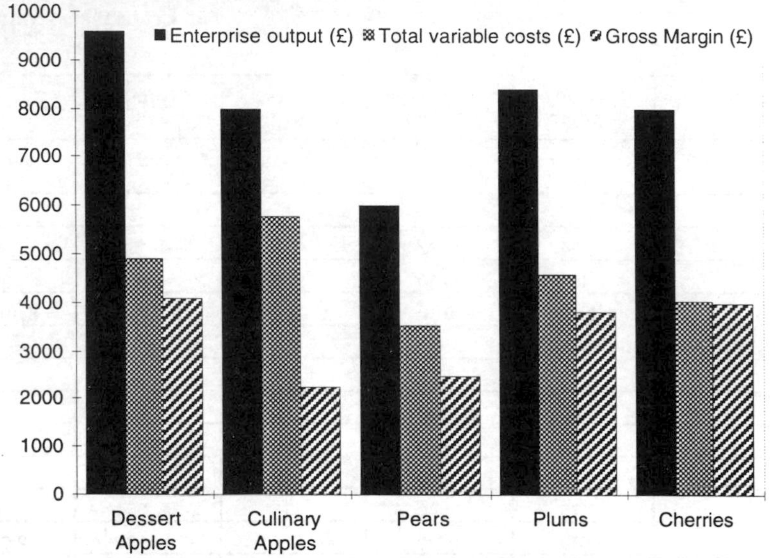
10000
9000
8000
7000
6000
5000
4000
3000
2000
1000
0
Enterprise output (£)
Total variable costs (£)
Gross Margin (£)
Dessert Apples
Culinary Apples
Pears
Plums
Cherries

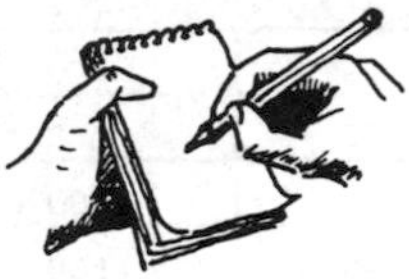

SPECIALIST SECTORS

C: FIELD VEGETABLES

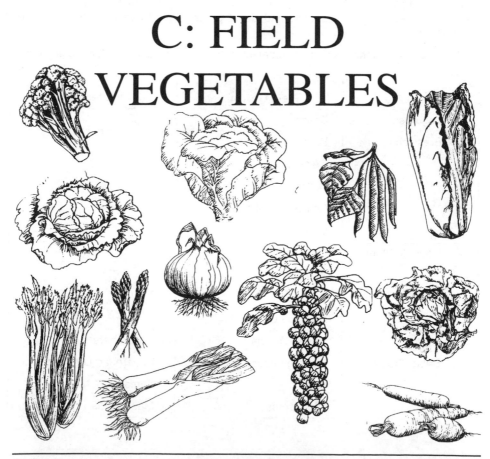

INTRODUCTION

VEGETABLES

Introduction

There are of course, a vast number of different vegetables grown both out of doors on a field scale and under controlled environmental conditions ('Protected') inside greenhouses be they made of glass or plastic film.

This Outsider's Guide has focussed on those vegetables which are of major commercial importance in the UK. This importance is reflected both in the direct value of output of each vegetable crop and in the value of business that this creates for those organisations supplying the needs of vegetable growers.

Examples of such service industries are banks, insurers, accountants, consultants and farm input suppliers, not forgetting the activities which underpin the success of the vegetatable sector - the research and development establishment and the training organisations.

This table summarises the main vegetables that are considered within these pages:

	Field Grown	Protected
Legumes	Beans	
Brassicas	Brussels Sprouts	
	Calabrese	
	Cabbage	
	Chinese Cabbage	
	Cauliflower	
Roots & Others	Carrots	
	Asparagus	
	Leeks	
	Dry Bulb Onions	
Salad Crops	Spring Onions	Cucumbers
	Iceberg Lettuce	Butterhead Lettuce
	Celery	Tomatoes
	Watercress	Mushrooms

LEGUMES

C: FIELD VEGETABLES

The crops discussed in this section are all grown outdoors on a field scale. Small quantities of some crops may also be grown under protection in order to extend the British season of availability.

PEAS

Peas are known to have been one of the earliest vegetables to be grown as they have been found in Stone Age dwellings in Switzerland. Peas have been grown and eaten in Britain over the centuries and were an important dried product, rich in protein and useful for thickening soups etc. throughout the winter when fresh produce was unavailable.

Today the majority of the crop grown for human consumption in the UK is frozen, the remainder being canned, dried or sold fresh on PYO farms. Recently demand has increased for 'mangetout' peas, though the high labour requirements for picking make this an expensive, luxury crop. Peas are being seriously researched as a potential food source in the novel food processing industry. Like broad beans, peas are grown on a field scale as a break crop which is sold as animal feed. The production and husbandry details are again discussed as a separate section 'Peas and Beans' in The Outsider's Guide to Crop Production.

BROAD BEANS

This is one of our oldest cultivated vegetables, which can be traced back to the 16th century. Broad beans are a hardy vegetable sown in November outside to overwinter as seedlings (some risk in severe winters) or sown as early in the spring as is possible (Feb - Mar). The crop is ready in June and along with strawberries provides a popular PYO alternative. The majority of the crop however, is split between the processing and fresh market.

The majority of the crop grown for human consumption goes for processing, only 25% is sold fresh. Broad beans are grown on a field scale as a break crop which is sold as animal feed. The production and husbandry details are discussed as a separate section 'Peas and Beans' in The Outsider's Guide to Crop Production.

DWARF / FRENCH BEANS

An ancient vegetable, the Dwarf French Bean is believed to have been imported into the UK from France during the reign of Elizabeth I. A delicacy for wealthy tables at that time, it has only recently become a commercial proposition.

In the UK, dwarf beans need heat , and some 5 hectares are grown under glass for the 'early' premium market. The majority late (season as of runner beans) outdoor crop (some 95%) is either canned or frozen. Only a small amount enters the fresh market.

BEANS

Husbandry conditions and Production Cycle for dwarf beans are very similar to those of runner beans, the main difference being that tall canes or similar construction are not needed for dwarf varieties.

Runner Beans

This crop originated in South America and arrived in the UK during the 17th century. The bean was grown as an ornamental until the 19th century when the wealthy began to eat the crop. Today the commercial crop goes to the fresh market. Grown on sticks as a climbing plant or pinched and allowed to trail, the crop is raised from seed and either transplanted from protection or sown direct into the seed bed in mid-May.

Runner beans are tropical plants and will only survive in the UK between periods of frost i.e. end May - late September. For this reason they are confined to being grown in the more favoured or sheltered areas of the UK. Harvesting is by hand and is labour intensive and some extension to the UK's short season is achieved by growing under polythene tunnels.

Availability from UK Producers

Jan	Feb	Mar	Apr	May	Jun	Jul	Aug	Sept	Oct	Nov	Dec
					▒	▒	▒	▒			

Availability from Overseas Producers

	Jan	Feb	Mar	Apr	May	Jun	Jul	Aug	Sept	Oct	Nov	Dec
Kenya	▒	▒	▒	▒	▒	▒	▒	▒	▒	▒	▒	▒
Spain				▒	▒							
Zimbabwe	▒	▒	▒							▒	▒	▒
Netherlands				▒	▒	▒	▒	▒	▒			

Key Facts

	Runner & Dwarf Beans	Broad Beans	Peas
Area Grown (ha)	4,786	2,695	46,160
Gross Production ('000t)	53.5	13.7	309.2
UK Market Size ('000t)	All beans 37.4		236.6
UK Market Share (%)	All beans 77.0		97.9
UK Exports ('000t)	All beans 8.6		7.8
UK Imports ('000t)	8.6	n/a	5.0

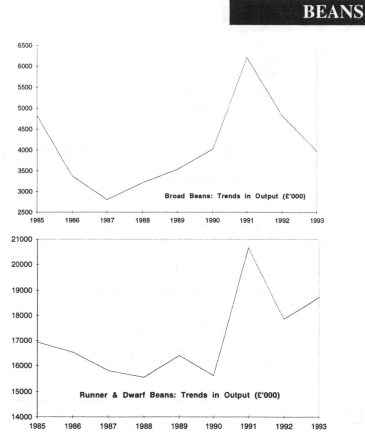

Broad Beans: Trends in Output (£'000)

Runner & Dwarf Beans: Trends in Output (£'000)

Grading Standards

Fine Beans:	Three classes: Extra, I and II
Beans Other:	Two classes I and II
Very fine:	Width of pod not exceeding 6 mm
Fine	Width of pod not exceeding 9 mm
Average	Width of pod exceeding 9 mm

Husbandry Summary

Varieties	Streamline, Enorma, Emergo, Prizewinner. Certified seed free from Halo Blight.
Soils	Deep well drained Grade 1 soil most suitable. Frost free site preferred with shelter.
Environment	Artificial screening (Paraweb) or Alder windbreaks used to improve microclimate. Irrigation is essential, with sufficient resource to apply

BRASSICAS

100-150mm/ha grown over the season. Drip or small droplet applicators ideal to maximise water resource.

Nutrition   Annual dressings of 225kg N, 150kg P, 100kg K are recommended per hectare following soil analysis.

Production Cycle

Sept - Oct   Following deep ploughing and cultivations 'baulk up' into 200 cm beds prior to next season. Bed formers may be used. Leave to overwinter. Desiccate weeds emerging. Apply base dressings.

Apr - Jun   Depending on earliness/lateness of site, field sow at 34 kg/ha in double rows 60 cm apart. Plant spacing in the row 30 cm. Final plant population 16500/ha. Apply herbicides (Trifluralin and Bentozone).

Jun +   Either erect permanent support system (post and wires) or install bamboo cane support system, or a combination of both. String up to support developing plants.

Apr - Sept   Irrigation applied dependent on prevailing weather conditions. Tensiometers are used to measure SMD's. Following crop set, SMD's kept to under 0.5mm 1250 x 1000 litres/ha required. Apply crop protection programme for the control of pests and diseases. Use Pirimicarb for aphid control.

Jul - Oct   Hand harvesting into either non-returnable market boxes (4.5kg, 6.3kg) for direct marketing, or into field crates for cooling and prepacking.

BRASSICAS

Introduction

Many of the crops in this family are derived from the wild cabbage, Brassica oleracea, which is native to the coastal cliffs of Britain. The plants are well suited to British soil and climate and have been selected, adapted and cultivated to produce widely differing races. They are all biennials and hardy under British winter conditions but commercially are grown as annuals.

BRUSSELS SPROUTS

This crop was sold in Belgium in the 13th century and was subsequently introduced into Britain, entering commercial production during the 19th century.

Cultivation is now split between the traditional direct sowing technique and transplants either from seedbeds or peat cells and blocks. About 75% of the crop is sold on the fresh market and is mostly still hand picked, whilst the rest for the freezing market is now mechanically harvested.

BRUSSELS SPROUTS

Availability from UK Producers

Jan	Feb	Mar	Apr	May	Jun	Jul	Aug	Sept	Oct	Nov	Dec
▓	▓	▓					▓	▓	▓	▓	▓

Availability from Overseas Producers

	Jan	Feb	Mar	Apr	May	Jun	Jul	Aug	Sept	Oct	Nov	Dec
Netherlands	▓	▓						▓	▓	▓	▓	▓

Key Facts

Area Grown (ha)	8,558
Gross Production ('000t)	128.8
UK Market Size ('000t)	114.91
UK Market Share (%)	98.4
UK Exports ('000t)	0.60
UK Imports ('000t)	1.81

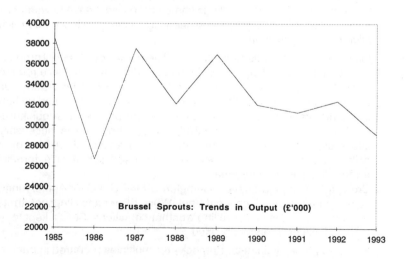

Brussel Sprouts: Trends in Output (£'000)

BRUSSELS SPROUTS

Grading Standards
Three classes: Class I, Class II and Class III

Class	I	II	III
Brussels Sprouts - trimmed	10mm	10mm	10mm+
Brussels Sprouts - untrimmed	15mm	15mm	10mm

Class I   difference between largest + smallest sprout in one package must not exceed 20mm.

Husbandry Summary

Varieties	Refer to commercial seed houses for latest Hybrid varieties.
Soils	Well drained Grade 1 soils, pH of 6.5 - 7.0 plus. Level sites preferred.
Environment	Irrigation is essential, with sufficient resource to apply 100 mm/ha over the season.
Nutrition	Annual dressings of 300kg N, 75kg P, 125kg K are recommended per hectare following soil analysis. Top dressing of 200kg N during season.

Production Cycle

Oct - Dec   Apply base dressings. Following deep ploughing and cultivations flat beds within 180cm wheelings can be prepared. Leave to weather over winter. Desiccate emerging weed seedlings. Lightly cultivate and roll back prior to planting in spring.

Feb - Apr   Plant out small block raised plants or modules raised by specialist propagator. Plant spacing 50 x 45cm - 75 x 50cm depending on sprout size required at harvest. Apply Propachlor, Tirfluralin and Desmetryne herbicides. Drilled crops can also be established using pelleted seed, and thinned by hand to final plant stand 50 x 31 - 45cm, if grown for processor or quick freezer employing single pass mechanical harvest. Irrigation is necessary for successful plant establishment. Anti-capping agents should be used on drilled crops to assist emergence. Trifluralin used as herbicide, Iprodine as a seed dressing for Alternaria.

May - Jul   Crop protection programmes: Demeton-S-methyl (x2) for Aphid, fungicidal sprays for Alternaria, Light Leaf Spot, White Blister and Ringspot. Irrigation applied, dependent on prevailing weather conditions. SMD's kept to under 0.5mm. Rain guns generally used.

June+   Harvest in 8.8kg field nets. Prepacks for multiples prepared in packhouse and distributed via coolchain.

CALABRESE

CALABRESE (BROCCOLI)

There is considerable confusion over nomenclature in Lincolnshire where the term Broccoli is used to describe spring cauliflowers. In 1986 the 12 leading UK growers formed the Broccoli Growers Association and agreed to use that title (Broccoli) on all packaging. The MAFF still use the term 'calabrese' in statistical analysis. NB: In 1987 the Broccoli Growers Association joined with the Brussels Sprout and Cauliflower Growers Association to form the Brassica Growers Association.

Broccoli is grown by successive sowing both outdoor and under protection in modules. Harvest takes place in the corresponding months of June to November. The production of Broccoli began in the UK only some 23 years ago (the plant originates from Italy). Since then considerable expansion has taken place with current production estimated at approximately 4,674 hectares.

Availability from UK Producers

Jan	Feb	Mar	Apr	May	Jun	Jul	Aug	Sept	Oct	Nov	Dec
					:::	:::	:::	:::	:::	:::	

Availability from Overseas Producers

	Jan	Feb	Mar	Apr	May	Jun	Jul	Aug	Sept	Oct	Nov	Dec
Belgium / Lux.				:::	:::	:::	:::	:::	:::	:::	:::	:::

Key Facts

Area Grown (ha)	6,270
Gross Production ('000t)	65.50
UK Market Size ('000t)	n/a
UK Market Share (%)	n/a
UK Exports ('000t)	n/a
UK Imports ('000t)	n/a

CALABRESE

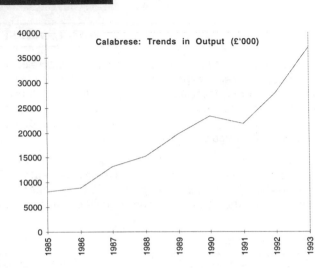

Calabrese: Trends in Output (£'000)

Grading Standards

None published.

Husbandry Summary

Varieties   Mercedes, Cruiser, Comet, SG1, RS1, Gem, Laser, Corvet, Skiff.

Soils   Well drained Grade 1 soils. pH of 6.5-7.0+. Level sites preferred.

Environment   Irrigation is essential, with sufficient resource to apply 100-150 mm/ha over the season.

Nutrition   Annual dressings of 250kg N, 60kg P, 150kg K, 45kg Mg per hectare are recommended following soil analysis.

Production Cycle

Oct - Dec   Apply base dressings. Following deep ploughing and cultivations 'baulk up' into beds prior to next season. Bed formers may be used. 180 cm wheel centres common. Leave to overwinter. Desiccate emerging weeds. Roll back prior to planting out or drilling.

Mar - Apr   From this time onwards, plant out small block raised plants or modules raised by specialist propagator. Plant density 8-10 plants/sq.m on 4 row beds between 180 cm wheel centres. Apply Propachlor. Early crops can be covered after 24 - 48 hours with 10 m plastic covers (500 holes/sq.m). Remove at 10-15 mm spear stage. Drilled crops can also be established using pelleted seed, and thinned by hand to final plant stand (12 sq.m). Sequential plantings and sowings (until July) provide continuity of harvest. Irrigation is essential for successful plant establishment. Anti-capping agents should be used on drilled crops to assist emergence.

CABBAGE

May - Jul	Late May, crop protection programmes - Demeton-S-methyl (x2). Cypermethrin and Chlorothalonil used. Cabbage Root Fly is a problem. Irrigation applied dependent on prevailing weather conditions. SMD's kept under 0.5mm. Rain guns generally used.
May - Nov	From late May, harvest into field crates. Vacuum cool or rapid cool prior to trimming, grading and packing. For the wholesale markets face packs in 7 kg cartons, often top iced, are used. Multiples require overwrapped pre-packs. In field pulverise crop prior to new cultivations.

CABBAGE

This crop is split into three periods of availability, spring, Summer and autumn and winter cabbage.

Some cabbage, especially the winter variety is imported from Holland. The origin of cabbage is uncertain though its cultivation is thought to date back to Roman times when it originated from the wild or sea cabbage.

Recent developments by plant breeders have produced a wealth of variation in leaf shape, size and texture. Production of all are by seed, now usually raised under glass in modules and transplanted into the field.

Availability from UK Producers

Jan	Feb	Mar	Apr	May	Jun	Jul	Aug	Sept	Oct	Nov	Dec

Availability from Overseas Producers

	Jan	Feb	Mar	Apr	May	Jun	Jul	Aug	Sept	Oct	Nov	Dec
Netherlands												

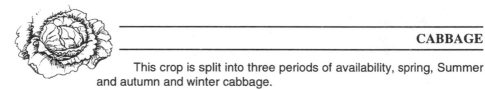

Key Facts

	spring	Summer	winter
Area Grown (ha)	5,762	6,943	7,587
Gross Production ('000t)	77.90	273.1	290.5
		All types	
UK Market Size ('000t)		592.08	
UK Market Share (%)		97.1	
UK Exports ('000t)		0.4	
UK Imports ('000t)		17.28	

CABBAGE

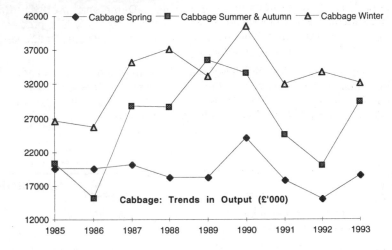

Cabbage: Trends in Output (£'000)

Legend: ◆ Cabbage Spring ■ Cabbage Summer & Autumn △ Cabbage Winter

Grading standards

2 Classes : I and II

Sizing determined by net weight -> 350 g per unit.

Sizing is compulsory for headed cabbage presented in packages. In that case the weight of the heaviest head in any one package must not be more than double the weight of the lightest head.

Husbandry Summary

Varieties	Summer cabbage: Green Express, Stonehead, Pedrillo and Apex.
	Spring: Myatts Offenham Compacta, Greensleeves, Early Market
	winter: Savoy, January King, Celtic, Tundra, Ice Prince.
Soils	Well drained Grade 1 and 2 soils, pH 6.5 - 7.0. Level sites preferred.
Environment	Irrigation is essential, with sufficient resource to apply 100mm/ha over the season.
Nutrition	Summer, autumn and winter: annual dressings of 150kg N, 125kg P, 250kg K per hectare are recommended following soil analysis. Top dressing of 150kg N during season.
	Spring: annual dressings of 50kg N, 60kg P and 190kgK plus 200kg N per hectare as top dressing.

OUTSIDER'S GUIDE

CHINESE CABBAGE

Production Cycle

Oct - Dec	Following deep ploughing and cultivations apply base fertiliser dressings. Raised or flat beds within 180 cm wheelings can be prepared. Leave to weather over winter. Desiccate emerging weed seedlings. Lightly cultivate, incorporating Trifluralin herbicide and roll back prior to sowing or planting in spring.
Apr - Jun	Summer Cabbage: sow with a precision drill to achieve, after singling, a plant stand at 500mm x 300mm. 5 rows per 1.5m bed, targeting 67,000 plants/ha. Apply Propachlor and Desmetryne herbicides post drilling. Transplants or modules are also used to establish.
May - Jul	Sow winter varieties in similar way.
Jul - Aug	Spring Cabbage: sow in rows 30-38cm (1.65kg/ha seed) recommended. Successional sowings made to give continuity of marketing. Transplants sometimes used, especially where year round production required.
May - Jul	Crop protection programmes applied - Aphid, Cabbage White Caterpillar, Cabbage Root Fly and Flea Beetle are the main pests. Clubroot, Downy and Powdery Mildews main diseases. Wetters are necessary due to waxy foliage. In some seasons and areas pigeon control necessary.
	Irrigation applied, particularly at establishment, dependent on prevailing weather conditions. SMD's kept to under 0.5mm. Rain guns generally used.
Jul - Nov	Hand harvest summer cabbage into boxes 13.6kg. Head weight between 0.75kg and 1.25kg according to season and variety grown.
Nov - Mar	(or year round). Harvest winter and spring cabbage into nets or 13.6kg cartons. Pack into field crates for transference to packhouse for pre-packing for multiples.

CHINESE CABBAGE

Chinese Leaves, Chinese Leaf and Chinese Cabbage are all names given to the same vegetable, which is a relatively new crop grown outdoors in Britain since 1980. This Brassica originates from Asia and Eastern China where it has been eaten since the 5th Century. It has rapidly gained popularity in Britain as an addition to salads when eaten raw or cooked as a stir-fry vegetable. It is also grown indoors in order to supply the early market during April and May.

Availability from UK Producers

Jan	Feb	Mar	Apr	May	Jun	Jul	Aug	Sept	Oct	Nov	Dec
			▓	▓	▓	▓	▓	▓	▓	▓	▓

CHINESE CABBAGE

Availability from Overseas Producers

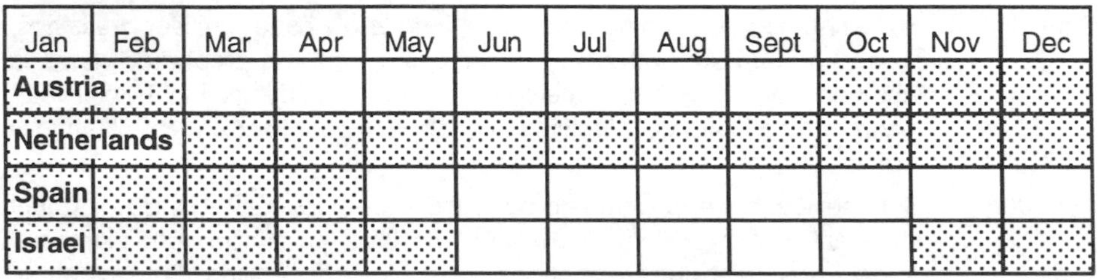
Jan
Feb
Mar
Apr
May
Jun
Jul
Aug
Sept
Oct
Nov
Dec
Austria
Netherlands
Spain
Israel

Key Facts

Area Grown (ha)	**420**
Gross Production ('000t)	**19.4**
UK Market Size ('000t)	**n/a**
UK Market Share (%)	**n/a**
UK Exports ('000t)	**n/a**
UK Imports ('000t)	**n/a**

Trends

No figures available from the Ministry.

CHINESE CABBAGE

Grading Standards

As for Cabbage

Husbandry Summary

Varieties	Kasumi (short barrel) types, Hobbit, Marquis, Parkin, Shinki.
Soils	Well drained mineral or peat soils, pH of 6.5-7.0+. Level sites preferred.
Environment	Irrigation is essential, with sufficient resource to apply 100-150mm/ha grown over the season. Harvest resources must be available, including vacuum cooling.
Nutrition	Annual dressings of 150kg N, 75kg P, 125kg K per hectare are recommended following soil analysis.

Production Cycle

Oct - Dec	Apply base dressings. Following deep ploughing and cultivations 'baulk up' into beds prior to next season. Bed formers may be used. 180cm wheel centres common. Leave to overwinter. Desiccate emerging weeds. Roll back prior to planting out or drilling.
Mar+	Plant out block raised plants (4.3cm) raised in heat by specialist propagator. Plant density 40cm x 40cm on 4 row beds between 180cm wheel centres. Apply Chlorpyrifos and Propachlor. Some mechanical hoeing may be necessary. Crop development should be 'even' to avoid 'bolting' or early flowering. Inter-row cultivations may be necessary. Crop growth is very rapid.
Jun - Jul	Using a precision drill and pelleted seed a later, drilled crop can be grown (for late harvest). Pre and post emergence herbicides used, plus irrigation to establish the crop. Crop protection programmes used - Demeton-S-methyl (x2). Benomyl, Iprodine (x2) and Deltamethrin (x3) are used. Irrigation applied dependent on prevailing weather conditions. SMD's kept to under 0.5mm. Rain guns generally used. Growth is rapid for drilled crop, producing a 1-1.5kg head within 2 months.
Jun - Nov	Harvest into field crates. Trim, grade and pack in packhouse into cardboard boxes in sleeved 12's. Prepacks into polybags for multiples. Vacuum cool to extend shelf life.
Sept - Oct	Harvest into bulk bins for storage. Carefully trim and pack into bins. Store at 4°C. Grade and pack from Nov to Feb. In field pulverise crop prior to new cultivations.

CAULIFLOWER

CAULIFLOWER

A vegetable, once only available to the rich, Cauliflower has been cultivated in the UK on a large scale since the 18th century. The plant originates from Southern Europe and is in fact a form of cabbage. Cultivation is concentrated in Lincolnshire and the UK imports cauliflower from France particularly during December to April.

Developments currently underway include the cultivation of disease resistance, and purple/green varieties e.g. Aston Purple (sometimes called Cape Broccoli).

An increased range of cauliflowers are now available in the supermarkets due to improved harvesting techniques. All Brassica crops are extremely susceptible to handling damage.

Availability from UK Producers

Jan	Feb	Mar	Apr	May	Jun	Jul	Aug	Sept	Oct	Nov	Dec
▓	▓	▓	▓	▓	▓	▓	▓	▓	▓	▓	▓

Availability from Overseas Producers

	Jan	Feb	Mar	Apr	May	Jun	Jul	Aug	Sept	Oct	Nov	Dec
France	▓	▓	▓	▓	▓					▓	▓	▓
Spain	▓	▓	▓							▓	▓	▓

Key Facts

Area Grown (ha)	19,860
Gross Production ('000t)	369.40
UK Market Size ('000t)	378.0
UK Market Share (%)	90.10
UK Exports ('000t)	3.00
UK Imports ('000t)	37.40

CAULIFLOWER

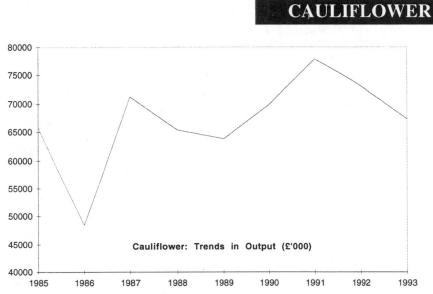

Cauliflower: Trends in Output (£'000)

Grading Standards

Classes : Extra, I, II and III

Sizing :   determined by maximum diameter of equatorial section or by the arc measurement on the largest dimension of the upper part of the inflorescence.

Minimum diameter 11cm OR Minimum dimension 13cm

Difference: between largest & smallest in package = 5cm arc, 4cm diameter (maximum).

Class III :

Min. diameter 9cm, arc 11cm (per package) and difference in package not greater than 6cm diameter, 7cm arc.

Husbandry Summary

Varieties   Summer: White Fox, White Summer, Dok Elgon, Revito, Plana.

Autumn: Wallaby, Dok Elgon, Snowy River, White Rock, Revito, Plana.

Soils   Grade 1 soils ideal, with water retention properties, pH 6.5 - 7.0, alkaline soils preferred.

Environment Irrigation is essential, with sufficient resource to apply 100mm/ ha over the season.

Nutrition   Annual dressings of 300kg N, 125kg P, 250kg K per ha are recommended following soil analysis.

CAULIFLOWER

Production Cycle

Oct - Dec	Following deep ploughing and cultivations apply base fertiliser dressings, flat beds within 180cm wheelings can be prepared. Leave to weather over winter. Desiccate emerging weed seedlings.
Mar - May	Plant out block raised plants or modular cell tray plants (308's) supplied by specialist propagator. Chlorpyrifos drench applied to modules preplanting for Cabbage Root Fly control. Desiccant herbicides (Paraquat or Glyphosate) used immediately prior to planting. Propachlor and Trifluralin herbicides applied pre and post planting.
	Planting density 60 x 60 x 60 x 45cm. to give 27,000 - 36,000 plants/ha. Some mechanical or hand hoeing may be necessary.
May +	Crop protection programme - Aphid control by Demeton-S-methyl and Caterpillar control by Cypermethrin.
Apr - Oct	Apply irrigation requirements, keeping SMD under 10mm.
Jul - Nov	Harvest as face packs direct into wooden, slatted field cartons. Multiple programme requires customer prepacks, individually label into their own outers etc. Mobile harvesting gantries common to cut, trim, pack in field. Cooling facilities ensure distribution below 8°C.
	For early summer production transplant 60mm block raised plants (from specialist propagators). Plant at 66 x 45 cm (3600/ha). Plants overwintered, with x 2 N top dressings of 100kg/ha. Harvest end May - end June. Pigeons can be a svere problem in certain areas.

ROOTS AND OTHER CROPS

Introduction

In this part, we look at a collection of four vegetables which are not naturally classified together, however they are put together here as they fall outside the other natural classifications of Brassica or Salad crops. These vegetables are Carrots, Asparagus, Leeks and finally Dry Bulb Onions.

'Roots' is a loose term used to group crops such as carrots, swedes, turnips, parsnips and beetroot etc. Carrots are by far the most important commercial crop so will be discussed in more detail.

CARROTS

Carrots originate from the wild carrot and have been developed over the centuries to produce the good variety in shape, colour, flavour and size that can be selected today. Carrots were first introduced into Britain into Kent and Surrey in quantity in the reign of Elizabeth I.

The UK is now Europe's largest producer of carrots and the crop represents some 17,880 hectares of production annually. The UK's success is largely the result of better growth systems allowing year round production, improved cultivation and organised producers marketing through co-operatives.

Current developments include the improvement of cultivars within commercial production, with breeding for disease resistant varieties being high on the agenda. Cultivars are currently being trialed for resistance to Powdery Mildew and Cavity Spot. Breeders are also starting to produce Carrot Fly resistant lines.

With the work of the British Carrot Growers Association the crop has been vigorously marketed throughout the EU and Sweden. Within the EU growers have sought exempted trader status, giving a class I sample (UK inspected) across all member states with no further certification required.

Availability from UK Producers

Jan	Feb	Mar	Apr	May	Jun	Jul	Aug	Sept	Oct	Nov	Dec
▓	▓	▓	▓	▓	▓	▓	▓	▓	▓	▓	▓

Availability from Overseas Producers

	Jan	Feb	Mar	Apr	May	Jun	Jul	Aug	Sept	Oct	Nov	Dec
France	▓	▓	▓	▓	▓	▓	▓	▓	▓	▓	▓	▓
Spain	▓											
Netherlands	▓	▓	▓	▓	▓	▓	▓	▓	▓	▓	▓	▓

CARROTS

Key Facts

Area Grown (ha)	17,880
Gross Production ('000t)	818.50
UK Market Size ('000t)	643.93
UK Market Share (%)	94.70
UK Exports ('000t)	8.32
UK Imports ('000t)	34.35

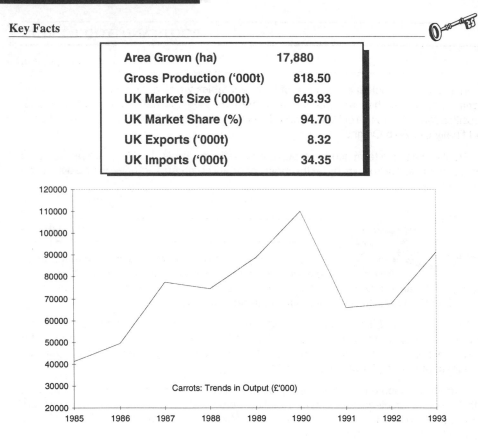

Carrots: Trends in Output (£'000)

Grading Standards

3 Classes: Extra, I and II. Sizing: max. diameter or weight without foliage.

a) Early carrots/small root varieties: Size = between 10mm and 40mm

b) Maincrop & large root varieties: Extra: 20-45mm or 50-200g,

Class I : 20-50mm or 50g-250g, Class II : Greater than either 20mm or 50g. There is only a minimum size requirement for this class.

Husbandry Summary

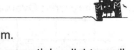

Varieties	Nantes, Autumn King or Chantenay types, Berlikum.
Soils	Organic peat soils, loamy peats or sands. Irrigation essential on lighter soil.
Environment	Avoid over-exposed sites. On sandy soils a 'nurse' cover crop of barley sown to prevent erosion, (later eliminated with Fusilade).

ASPARAGUS

Irrigation is essential, with sufficient resource to apply 100 mm -150 mm/ha grown over the season.

Nutrition Annual dressing of 60kg N, 200kg P, 100kg K per hectare are recommended following soil analysis. Some trace element applications may be necessary on light soils.

Production Cycle

Oct - Dec Apply base dressings. Following deep ploughing and cultivations 'baulk up' into beds prior to next season. Bed formers may be used. 180cm wheel centres common. Leave to overwinter. Desiccate emerging weeds. Roll back prior to drilling.

Jan - Feb Depending on earliness of site field sow at 80-150 seeds/sq.m in single scattered rows 44cm apart, or twin rows at 70cm apart if field stored. (2.5 million seeds/ha). Cover with perforated polythene film. Remove early/mid May.

Mar - May Continue main crop drilling in sequence. Herbicides (Linuron and Metoxuron) applied. Carbofuran granules applied with drillings against Carrot Fly. Inter row cultivations may be necessary.

Mar + Irrigation applied dependent on prevailing weather conditions. SMD's kept to under 0.5mm. Rain guns generally used, applying abstracted water from streams/dykes/boreholes. Apply crop protection programme for the control of pests and diseases. Use Pirimicarb for Aphid control. Carrot Fly controlled by applications of Triazophos (x3) or Quinalphos during Aug/Sept Metaylaxyl plus Manoozeb used for control of Cavity Spot.

Jun - winter Harvest using mechanical filters and trailers. Transport to washer, sizer, and quality grader. 12.5kg paper sacks used for wholesale market. Prepacks into polybags for multiples.

ASPARAGUS

Introduction

Asparagus, which is a member of the lily family, was known in Ancient Greek and Roman times, and has been grown in English gardens since at least the 16th Century.

It has been grown commercially for hundreds of years in Britain and current producers are members of The Aparagus Growers' Association. Members are enthusiastic about carrying out Research and Development into crop improvement in order to compete with imports which extend the rather short British season. Freshness is an important factor and obviously favours home-produced high quality supplies.

Asparagus shoots are produced annually from a perennial crown which has a life-span of 10-20 years.

ASPARAGUS

Availability From UK Producers

Jan	Feb	Mar	Apr	May	Jun	Jul	Aug	Sept	Oct	Nov	Dec
				░░░	░░░						

Availability From Overseas Producers

	Jan	Feb	Mar	Apr	May	Jun	Jul	Aug	Sept	Oct	Nov	Dec
USA	░░	░░	░░	░░	░░	░░						
Spain		░░	░░	░░	░░							

Key Facts

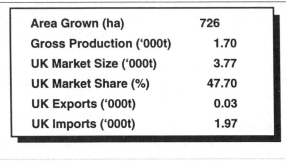

Area Grown (ha)	**726**
Gross Production ('000t)	**1.70**
UK Market Size ('000t)	**3.77**
UK Market Share (%)	**47.70**
UK Exports ('000t)	**0.03**
UK Imports ('000t)	**1.97**

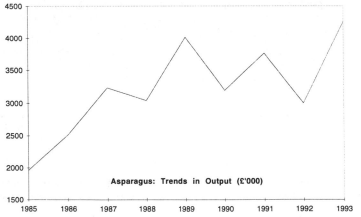

Asparagus: Trends in Output (£'000)

Grading Standards

New regulations not yet published.

ASPARAGUS

Husbandry Summary

Varieties	Male varieties are preferred: Boonlim, Geynlim and Franklim, hybrids e.g. Cito & some French available.
Soils	Medium loams, well-drained, frost-free site, pH 6.2-6.5.
Environment	Irrigation is essential, particularly for crop establishment, and with sufficient resource to apply 80 - 100mm/ha over the season, keeping SMD within 15-20mm.
Nutrition	Following initial soil analysis, 40kg N, 65kg P and 120kg K per hectare applied in establishment year. Annual dressings of 120kg N, 80kg P, 120kg K per ha recommended. Top dressings of 2 x 55kg N annually.

Production Cycle

June+	Site should be fallowed, applying Glyphosate to perennial weeds when at maximum foliage. Deep sub-soiling in dry conditions, ploughing and cultivations prior to 'baulking' (with potato ridging body) prior to winter to create a ridged field profile. Apply base fertiliser dressings.
Feb	Plants should be raised by specialist propagators. Multicell trays (104's) used to produce modular well rooted young crowns. The ridged field must be kept clean using contact herbicides.
Mar	If using one year old crowns, plant out before bud growth commences to avoid risk of crown damage. Spacing as for modules (below).
June	Modules should be planted in rows 1.3-1.5m apart, setting the crowns 30cm in the row, about 10-12cm deep in the furrow base. Plant population 25,000/ha.
	Irrigate crop to establish and produce optimum quality of 'fern' to build crown size. Hand hoeing or carefully applied spot applications of contact herbicides may be necessary to keep plants weed-free.
Year 2&3	Control weeds using herbicides. MCPA applied at standard times. Very few pest and diseases but Asparagus Beetle controlled by approved pesticides. Do not harvest until 3rd year after planting. Cut down foliage in autumn when changes colour.
Apr - Jun	Harvest by hand. Asparagus stems cut 15-20cm using sharp blade inserted into bed soil. Uniform bundles graded to EU standards. 3.5-4.5 /ha is average range.
	Supermarkets require their own packaging, including over-wrapped trays packed into plastic crates. Cool chain distribution at <8°C is required. The wholesale market takes asparagus in cardboard outers, 0.25kg and 0.5kg bundles. Specialist catering trade and processors also supplied.

LEEKS

LEEKS

Introduction

Leeks are becoming an increasingly more important vegetable crop in the UK due to supermarket demand for year-round continuity of supply. Trials are being carried out to extend the season and close the summer gap, by growing early crops under polythene and improving storage conditions for leeks lifted in the spring.

Leek growing is a serious hobby in the North East of England where there is keen competition amongst exhibitors at shows to produce the largest and best leek. The British Leek Growers' Association was formed in 1985 in order that members might promote leeks and increase production and quality.

Availability from UK Producers

Jan	Feb	Mar	Apr	May	Jun	Jul	Aug	Sept	Oct	Nov	Dec
░	░	░	░			░	░	░	░	░	░

Availability from Overseas Producers

	Jan	Feb	Mar	Apr	May	Jun	Jul	Aug	Sept	Oct	Nov	Dec
Holland	░	░	░	░	░	░	░	░	░	░	░	░
France	░	░	░	░	░	░	░	░	░	░	░	░

Key Facts

Area Grown (ha)	3,411
Gross Production ('000t)	75.80
UK Market Size ('000t)	75.90
UK Market Share (%)	95.40
UK Exports ('000t)	0.07
UK Imports ('000t)	3.40

LEEKS

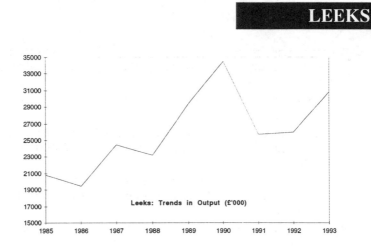

Leeks: Trends in Output (£'000)

Grading Standards

3 Classes : I, II and III

Sizing : determined by the diameter measured at right angles to the axis above the swelling of the neck.

Min: 8mm (early leeks) 10mm (others)

Class I : difference in the bundle: largest leek must not be more than twice the diameter of the smallest.

Husbandry Summary

Varieties   Selected according to season of marketing. Based on Autumn Mammoth-Argenta, Autumn Mammoth-Herwina, Giant winter Catalina & Autumn Mammoth-Snowstar types.

Sites & soils   Well drained Grade 1 medium loams ideal.

Environment   Irrigation is desirable with sufficient resource to apply 80-90mm/ ha over the season.

Nutrition   Annual dressings of 180kg N, 80kg P, 180kg K are recommended following soil analysis.

Production Cycle

Oct - Dec   Following deep ploughing and cultivation apply base fertiliser dressings. Raised beds within 180cm wheelings are prepared. Leave to weather over winter. Desiccate emerging weed seedlings with Paraquat.

Jan - Feb   Early crop - sow modules or multiseeded blocks 2 seeds / module, under protection.

Mar - Apr   Transplant early crop 75,000 modules/ ha at 45-60cm rows 10-15 cm apart in row. Plant population varies between 100,000-200,000 plants/ ha depending on variety and market. Apply Propachlor, Chlorthyl-dimethyl and Monolinuron herbicides.

DRY BULB ONIONS

For drilled crop - precision drill using 3.75 -4kg/ ha dressed seed in rows 45cm apart placing seed 5cm apart in row. 3-4 rows per bed depending on

market specification. Propachlor, Chlorthyl -dimethyl and Chlorbufam herbicides used.

Apr - May   Sow later crops into modules and transplant June- mid July.Bareroot transplants are less commonly used commercially at 150,000/ ha.Irrigate to establish.

May +   Apply crop protection programme. White Rot, Neck Rot and Rust are principal diseases. Apply Triademefon, Fenpropimorph or Ferbam/Maneb/ Zineb mix (x3).

Apr - Aug   Apply irrigation requirements keeping SMD under 10mm. Crop may be earthed up depending on market requirements.

Sept -Apr   Start harvest, following continuity of drillings and plantings and sequence of varieties. Single blade undercutters used on bed systems. For the wholesale market 6.35kg field crates used (4-5000 crates/ ha). More

stringent specifications required by multiples, requiring harvesting into field crates, carting to packhouse, trimming and prepacking. Cool chain distribution necessary. Processing market also important (soups).

DRY BULB ONIONS

Main areas of production are Lincolnshire, Norfolk, Cambridgeshire, Suffolk and Kent. The crop is grown on a field scale for mechanical harvesting and controlled storage.

The main types of production are: sowing direct into the field in spring; raising under glass in peat blocks (5 seeds per block) for transplanting in spring and finally planting as sets. The latter two provides earlier harvesting. A final production method is to sow in August using Japanese varieties which overwinter to harvest the following June-August. The first method of production provide for a harvest which begins in late August. From harvest the bulbs are stored in temperature/humidity controlled stores up to marketing during the spring. Some crop is held in cold store for sale during the following Summer. The UK therefore enjoys a year round supply of home produced onions.

Onions are imported from many countries including Spain, Eastern Europe, Israel and Italy. Much work is being undertaken to improve cultivars used for the Dry Bulb industry. Priorities include White Rot resistance and extending the storage life without applying suppressants.

Availability from UK Producers

Jan	Feb	Mar	Apr	May	Jul	Jul	Aug	Sept	Oct	Nov	Dec

OUTSIDER'S GUIDE

DRY BULB ONIONS

Availability from Overseas Producers

	Jan	Feb	Mar	Apr	May	Jun	Jul	Aug	Sept	Oct	Nov	Dec
Spain		▓	▓	▓	▓	▓	▓	▓	▓	▓	▓	▓
Netherlands		▓										
New Zealand			▓	▓	▓	▓	▓	▓				
Australia		▓	▓	▓	▓	▓	▓					

Key Facts

Area Grown (ha)	**7,699**
Gross Production ('000t)	**299.00**
UK Market Size ('000t)	**484.30**
UK Market Share (%)	**55.20**
UK Exports ('000t)	**8.38**
UK Imports ('000t)	**217.18**

Onions Dry Bulb: Trends in Output (£'000)

Grading Standards

3 Classes : I, II and III;

Sizing: diameter minimum differences in package must not exceed:

DRY BULB ONIONS

Difference	Diameter
5 mm	> 10 mm <20 mm
10 mm	>15 mm<25 mm
15 mm	>20 mm < 40 mm
20 mm	>40 mm <70 mm
30 mm	70 mm

Class III: maximum difference in size no more than 30mm.

Husbandry Summary

Varieties	Rijnsburger and F1 hybrids
Soils	Grade 1 sandy loams or stone free silts ideal.
Environment	Irrigation is essential, with sufficient resource to apply 100 mm/ha over the season. Cereal strips can be sown or planted to prevent soil erosion pre/post drilling on peaty/sandy soils.
Nutrition	Annual dressing of 90kg N, 150kg P, 125kg K per hectare are recommended following soil analysis.

Production Cycle

Oct - Dec	Following deep ploughing and cultivations apply base fertiliser dressings. Flat or raised beds within 180 cm wheelings can be prepared. Leave to weather overwinter. Desiccate emerging weed seedlings.
Feb	For transplanted crops, sow modules or blocks at 4-6 seeds/cell.
Apr	Plant out at 87,500 - 115,000/ha. Apply Chloridazon plus Chlorbufam post planting (or other compounds depending on soil type and weed spectrums). Some mechanical or hand hoeing may be necessary.
Mar	Direct drill 60-75 plants/sq. m in rows 30cm apart. 30-45cm on peaty soils. Apply Propachlor, Chlorthal-dimethyl, Chloridazon plus Chlorbufam herbicides (others may be necessary for different soil types and weed profiles).
May +	Crop protection programme - Aldicarb used for pest control (Eelworm)
Apr - Aug	Apply irrigation requirements, keeping SMD under 10mm.
Aug	For overwintered crop sow Japanese hybrids 60-90 plants/sq. m. Multi-seeded modules may also be used planted mid Sept. Peat/mineral soils preferred. Irrigation essential for establishment.
Aug - Sep	Harvest transplanted and direct drilled crop. Crop wind-rowed to dry and carted for drying and storage. Maleic hydrazide used to suppress shoots in store. Following grading crop sold in 25kg nets or in prepacks for multiples (0.5 or 1.0kg bags). Onions can be stored for 5-6 months. Overwintered crop harvested in June-August and sold direct without storage.

SPRING ONIONS

SALAD CROPS: SPRING ONIONS

The majority of green or spring onions are grown in Kent and the vale of Evesham.

Green onions are produced by a succession of sowings followed by harvesting and marketing. Traditional cultivars such as White Lisbon are now being challenged by Japanese cultivars which give an easier year round production. From this succession of sowing year round production can be achieved except in exceptionally severe winters.

Availability from UK Producers

Jan	Feb	Mar	Apr	May	Jul	Jul	Aug	Sept	Oct	Nov	Dec

Availability From Overseas Producers

	Jan	Feb	Mar	Apr	May	Jun	Jul	Aug	Sept	Oct	Nov	Dec
Cyprus												

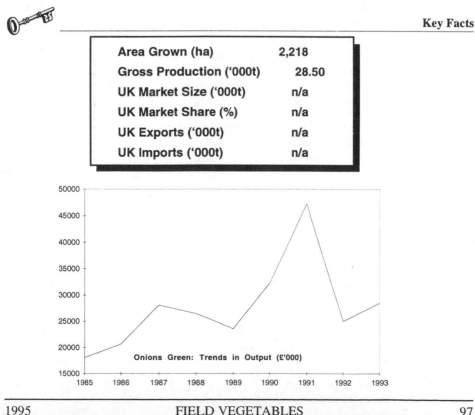

Key Facts

Area Grown (ha)	**2,218**
Gross Production ('000t)	**28.50**
UK Market Size ('000t)	**n/a**
UK Market Share (%)	**n/a**
UK Exports ('000t)	**n/a**
UK Imports ('000t)	**n/a**

Onions Green: Trends in Output (£'000)

OUTSIDER'S GUIDE

SPRING ONIONS

Grading Standards
None published.

Husbandry Summary

Varieties   spring sown: White Lisbon. Summer sown: Kyoto, Kikari, Ishiko - all Japanese varieties. Late summer sown: White Lisbon selections - winter Hardy.

Soils   Well drained Grade 1 loamy sands. Level sites preferred.

Environment   Irrigation is essential, with sufficient resource to apply 100mm/ha over the season.

Nutrition   Annual dressings of 75kg N, 200kg P, 75kg K per hectare are recommended following soil analysis. Top dressing of 200kg N/ha during season.

Production Cycle

Oct - Dec   Apply base dressings. Following deep ploughing and cultivations flat or raised beds within 180cm wheelings can be prepared. Leave to weather over winter. Desiccate emerging weed seedlings. Lightly cultivate and roll back prior to planting in spring.

Feb - Jul   Sow 8-12kg/ha ungraded seed with a precision drill on a 5cm band. Single rows 30cm apart, 5 rows per 1.5m bed, 100-125 seeds/m run. Seed dressed with Iodofanphos for Onion Fly control. Vinclozolin applied as a seed treatment or banded on crop emergence against White Rot. Herbicides recommended are Paraquat pre-emergence, Propachlor and Pendimethalin. Spot treatment also recommended. Successional sowings made to give continuity of marketing.

May - Jul   Crop protection programmes applied. Irrigation applied, dependent on prevailing weather conditions. SMD's kept to under 0.5 mm. Rain guns generally used, 227x1000ha budgeted.

Jul - Sept   Sow 10-15 kg/ha on a 5 cm band. Densities as above. This crop is overwintered to harvest the following April - June. 226kg/ha N, 125kg/ha P and 75kg/ha K required.

June +   For spring sown crop; Hand harvest into trays, 20 bunches/tray (10-15 onions weighing 140gm/bunch). Washing is usual. For multiples trimming and preparation into pre-packs in packhouse with cooling facilities.

ICEBERG LETTUCE

ICEBERG LETTUCE

Lettuce is an ancient vegetable, believed to have been introduced into Britain by the Romans. It has been recommended for its medicinal and herbal properties throughout the centuries.

During the last decade tremendous changes have been experienced in salad vegetables. Demand has increased considerably and UK producers have risen to meet the challenge of year round availability from imported produce.

A wide range of varieties are now available and the majority of the crop is field grown. 'Iceberg' is a term refering to a type of crisp lettuce rather than a specific variety and accounts for 75-80% of the total lettuce market. The British Iceberg Growers' Association, formed in 1984, aims to co-ordinate the production, marketing and research of the Iceberg lettuce. There have been problems in cultivation and achievement of top quality Iceberg production, but due to successful advances in technology, home-grown Iceberg is being exported.

The main Iceberg production areas are Kent, Lancashire, Cambridgeshire, Lincolnshire and Norfolk. Some protected crops are grown in Humberside, Lancashire and West Sussex.

Round or Butterhead lettuce is grown mostly in glasshouses in order to achieve year-round British lettuce supplies. Some round lettuce is grown outside in traditional market-garden areas during favourable weather conditions. Most outdoor crops are raised from seed sown in peat blocks or cell trays under glass and transplanted while the plants are small. Lettuce is highly susceptible to disease so constant research is being carried out to breed disease-resistant varieties.

Availability from UK Producers

Jan	Feb	Mar	Apr	May	Jul	Jul	Aug	Sept	Oct	Nov	Dec
				▓	▓	▓	▓	▓	▓		

Availability from Overseas Producers

	Jan	Feb	Mar	Apr	May	Jul	Jul	Aug	Sept	Oct	Nov	Dec
France		▓	▓	▓	▓					▓	▓	
Netherlands	▓	▓	▓	▓	▓	▓	▓	▓	▓	▓	▓	▓
Spain	▓	▓	▓	▓	▓						▓	▓
USA	▓	▓	▓		▓						▓	▓

ICEBERG LETTUCE

Key Facts

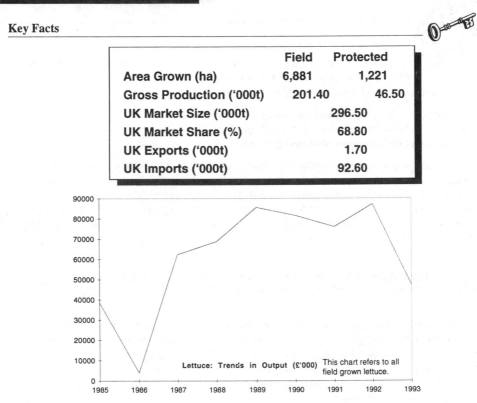

	Field	Protected
Area Grown (ha)	6,881	1,221
Gross Production ('000t)	201.40	46.50
UK Market Size ('000t)		296.50
UK Market Share (%)		68.80
UK Exports ('000t)		1.70
UK Imports ('000t)		92.60

Lettuce: Trends in Output (£'000) This chart refers to all field grown lettuce.

Grading Standards

These standards apply to:

all Lettuce, Curled Leaves Endives, Broad Leaves, (Batavian) Endives.

3 Classes I, II and III.

Sizing: by minimum weight & uniformity

Classes I and II	Open	Under Protection
Lettuce (excluding Iceberg)	150g	100g
Iceberg	300g	200g
Curled-leaved etc.	200g	150g
Class III		
Lettuce	>80g	>80g
Curled etc.	>100g	>100g

Uniformity:

Lettuce
Difference must not exceed:
40g for lettuce <150g per unit
100g for lettuce 150g - 300g
150g for lettuce 300g - 450g
300g for lettuce > 450g

Husbandry Summary

Varieties	Saladin, Kelvin, Malika. Other crisphead varieties like Great Lakes, Crispino.
Soils	Well drained Grade 1 and 2 soils are suitable. Mineral soils can be used. Sandy loams are ideal, pH 6.5-7.0 Liming may be necessary.
Planting	The use of raised beds in vegetable culture (between180 cm wheelings) has determined plant populations of 40,000-55,000 plants/ha (4/5 rows/bed). Bed length is often determined by irrigation reel length (200m). Iceberg can be grown on flat beds. 60-75% recovery at harvest i.e. 35,000-40,000 heads/ha. Hectarage planted will depend on harvest capacity, yield and cooling capacity.
Environment	Level sites with level raised beds allow for accurate planting and mechanical hoeing. Fleece covers for earliness spread the harvest season. Irrigation is essential, with sufficient resource to apply 100-150mm/ha grown over the season.
Nutrition	Annual dressings of 125kg N, 250kg P, 100kg K, and 50kg Mg per hectare are recommended following soil analysis. Top dressing using direct placement equipment gives maximum response at frame building stage. 30-40 units/ha N (Calcium nitrate often used). Nitrogen is freely available in soils at 20°C during June - August. Liquid fertiliser injection beside plant rows from March - June improves head weight and shortens period to maturity.

Production Cycle

Jul - Oct	Following deep ploughing and cultivations 'baulk up' into raised beds prior to next season. Bed formers may be used. Leave to overwinter. Desiccate weeds emerging continuously. Beds can be lightly cultivated and rolled pre-planting.
Mar - Jun	Sequential modular plantings to generate programmed production. Specialist plant propagators supply 13cm peat blocks or plug plants for mechanical planting. First plantings take 90 days to mature. Fleece covers (Agryl) can be used on early plantings to advance maturity by 7-14 days. Later plantings

CELERY

take 35-60 days to mature. Direct precision drilling is possible for mid season production, where specific weights and sizes are required. Pre and post planting herbicides are used. Limited products are available. Stale seed and raised beds are successful. Thermodormancy will occur at 27°C+. Early sites can be cropped twice.

Mar - Oct	Mechanical hoeing using a straddle tool bar or rotary brush may be necessary. A 7-day crop protection programme is recommended. Aphid and Thrip control, plus Mildew and Botrytis, has to be maintained. Lettuce Root Aphid emerges in mid season, and can decimate crops. Vigilant spraying is necessary.
Apr - Sept	Irrigation may be necessary pre and post planting, dependent on prevailing weather conditions. 7-10mm to assist establishment, 10-25mm at frame building, head formation and pre harvest may be necessary. Rain guns, crop booms or self propelled gantry irrigation lines are used.
May - Oct	Mobile field harvesting rigs can be used. Heads are trimmed, wrapped, sealed, labelled and cased in the field. Teams of cutters, wrappers and packers work alongside a carting trailer. Packed lettuce is vacuum cooled to achieve an internal temperature of 3-6°C, and introduced into 'coolchain' distribution. The alternative system is to field cut into crates and cart to central packhouse.

CELERY

Introduction

Celery is derived from the wild bitter-tasting plant 'smallage', native to Britain and other countries, which was used for its medicinal properties. It has been cultivated since the 18th century to produce the crop which is enjoyed today. Most of the home-produced crop is field grown around Ely in Cambridgeshire, Lancashire and Greater Manchester. Some glasshouse production occurs in Sussex, Essex, Suffolk and Cambridgeshire, but cheap imported self-blanching celery imposes close competition with producers of the protected crop.

Availability from UK Producers

Jan	Feb	Mar	Apr	May	Jul	Jul	Aug	Sept	Oct	Nov	Dec
						░	░	░	░		

Availability from Overseas Producers

	Jan	Feb	Mar	Apr	May	Jun	Jul	Aug	Sept	Oct	Nov	Dec
Spain	░	░	░	░							░	░
USA	░	░	░	░							░	░
Israel	░	░	░	░							░	░
Italy	░	░	░	░							░	░

OUTSIDER'S GUIDE

Key Facts

	Field Grown	Protected
Area Grown (ha)	**1046**	**163**
Gross Production ('000t)	**57.30**	**13.30**
UK Market Size ('000t)	**72.2**	
UK Market Share (%)	**56.5**	
UK Exports ('000t)	**1.5**	
UK Imports ('000t)	**31.4**	

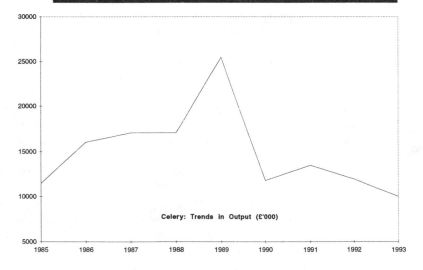

Celery: Trends in Output (£'000)

Grading Standards

2 classes : I and II. Uniformity required for class I

Sizing : minimum 150g

		(Per Package) Weight Variation Permitted
Class I	large 800 g	200 g
Class II	medium 500 g - 800g	150 g
Class III	small 150 g - 500g	100 g

OUTSIDER'S GUIDE

CELERY

Husbandry Summary

Varieties	Selected according to season of marketing. Celebrity, Ely White, Fenlander, Jason, Multipac, New Dwarf White.
Soils	Peat or loamy peat.
Environment	Irrigation is essential, particularly for crop establishment, and with sufficient resource to apply 80-100mm/ ha over the season, keeping SMD within 15-20mm.
Nutrition	Annual dressings of 150kg N, 100kg P, 250kg K per ha are recommended on organic soils following initial soil analysis.

Production Cycle

Oct - Dec	Following deep ploughing and cultivations apply base fertiliser dressings. Flat beds within 180cm wheelings are prepared. Leave to weather over winter. Desiccate emerging weed seedlings with Paraquat or other desiccants.
Jan - Feb	Specialist plant raisers sow modular blocks (1.5 - 4.3cm) or multicell plastic modular celltrays in heat (16°C+ to avoid bolting) and grown on under protection.
Apr - Jun	Plant out transplanted crop 30cm x 30cm, 110,000-115,000 modules/ha. Prometryne and two applications of Linuron herbicide applied. Irrigate to establish. Mechanical inter-row cultivations or row-brushing may be necessary.
Apr +	Apply irrigation requirements, keeping SMD under 10mm. Where crop grown on mineral soils apply additional 80kg/ha N.
May +	Apply crop protection programme: Phorate granules against Celery Fly (can be incorporated into module compost), Dimeton-s-methyl against Aphids. Carrot Fly can be a problem. Apply Benomyl and Chlorothalonil against fungal diseases such as Leaf Spot.
Aug - Nov	Harvest, following continuity of plantings and sequences of varieties. Crop cut into field crates, carting to packhouse for trimming, washing and packing. For the wholesale market crop usually sleeved into polythene outers, packed into cardboard cartons, 20-24 heads/carton. Wooden slatted crates are used. Vacuum cooling is desirable to extend shelf life. For multiple customers follow specifications. Cool chain distribution necessary (5-8°C). Processing market also important (soups).

WATERCRESS

WATERCRESS

Introduction

Watercress has not only been respected for its healing properties from early times, but also enjoyed as a food over the centuries. Watercress is found growing wild in streams, brooks and watermeadows, but cultivation of the crop in Britain started in the early 19th Century.

Now, due to modern technology, watercress is available throughout the year, as winter beds can be protected by plastic covers to guarantee supplies in frosty weather. Pure, fast flowing water is essential for healthy watercress so the main areas of production follow the chalk belt from Dorset and Wiltshire, through Hampshire (chief producing county) and the Home Counties.

Key Facts

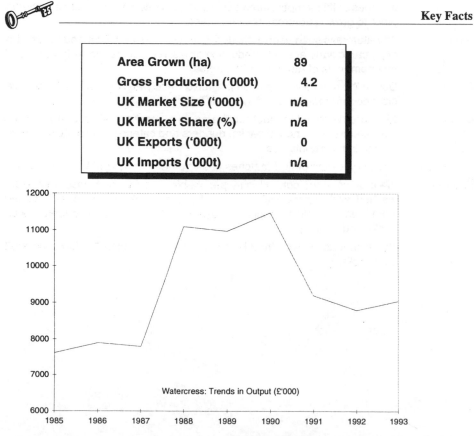

Area Grown (ha)	89
Gross Production ('000t)	4.2
UK Market Size ('000t)	n/a
UK Market Share (%)	n/a
UK Exports ('000t)	0
UK Imports ('000t)	n/a

Watercress: Trends in Output (£'000)

WATERCRESS

Grading Standards

None published for this crop.

Husbandry Summary

Since watercress is a specialist crop, confined to limited areas of production, and grown in water rather than soil, husbandry will not be detailed in the conventional style. Points for consideration and general notes will dictate the format for husbandry and production cycle for this crop.

Water — Water requirements are 5-10 million litres/ha/day consequently growers rely on water rising from natural springs and boreholes.

Temperature — Minimum temperature for growth 10.6°C. Water from underground aquifers emerges at this temperature year round. Air temperature must be higher in order to grow watercress above water level.

Seed — All watercress seed used in the UK is home-produced. Demand for seed is high, particularly at peak production times. 100,000 seeds weigh 28g and requirement is of the order of 5 tonnes.

Cycle — During the summer, crop span is approximately 28 days, so beds must be cleaned and replanted swiftly and efficiently.

Layout — Beds are designed to meet requirements of mechanical harvesters which cut watercress for pouch packs, punnets and catering packs. Some hand-harvesting still continues.

Harvesting — Peak harvesting period matches peak demand from April to September.

Distribution — Watercress, once cut, is highly perishable. It is hydro or vacuum-cooled, washed and transported via cool chain, packed on ice. Most bunched watercress is sold through wholesale markets. Multiples supply pouch packs and punnets.

Some imports, notably from Portugal, boost UK supplies during prolonged cold spells.

OUTSIDER'S GUIDE

FIELD VEGETABLES 1: FINANCIAL INFORMATION

	Legumes	Brassicas		
Enterprise **Item**	**Runner** **Beans**	**Cabbages**	**Cauliflower**	**Calabrese**
Production & Marketing				
Total UK hectares	4,786	20,292	19,860	6,270
Est. producer numbers	n/a	n/a		
Average unit size (ha)	50 - 200	15 - 100		
Average yield	depends on crop (see below under gross margins)			
Marketing channels	Grower Co-operatives. Large independent packhouses. Wholesale markets, supermarkets, processors, some direct sales via farm shops/PYO			
Investment Considerations				
Typical investment (£ /ha)		see note a		
Minimum size of Unit (ha)	20	10		
Lead time to 1st crop	weeks			
Production cycles /yr	continuous			
Cycles per year	1	1-2		
Rotational details	soil borne diseases			

a   Field harvest rigs cost £10 - £15,000

Gross Margins

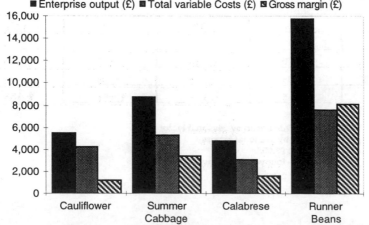

■ Enterprise output (£) ■ Total variable Costs (£) ▨ Gross margin (£)

SUMMARY

GROSS MARGINS

Enterprise Item	Cauliflower	Summer Cabbage	Calabrese	Runner Beans
Example variety	White Summer, White Fox, Dok, Elgon, Plana	Green Express, Stonehead, Pedrillo	Laser , Corvette, Cruiser, Skiff	Enorma Prize Winner, Emergo
OUTPUT				
Yield per hectare (tonnes unless otherwise stated)[a]	2,000 x 12's	3,500 x 13.6 kg	1,200 x 5 kg	21
Price/Unit of sale (£)[b]	2.75	2.50	4.00	750
Enterprise output (£)	**5,500**	**8,750**	**4,800**	**15,750**
VARIABLE COSTS (£) - Production				
Fertilisers	190	186	155	136
Sprays	40	148	130	97
Establishment seeds / plants	290	400	260	225
Water		10	10	250
Sundries				405[d]
Direct casual labour [c]	125	75	175	588
Subtotal production	**645**	**819**	**630**	**1,701**
VARIABLE COSTS (£) - Marketing				
Packing & cooling	1,300	1,575	686[e]	886
Transport & handling	900	1,750	336	963
Harvesting packing - casual labour[c]	870	300	1000	2,470
Commission	550	875	480	1,575
Drying and storage	-	-	-	-
Subtotal marketing	**3,620**	**4,500**	**2,502**	**5,894**
Total variable Costs (£)	4,265	5,319	3,132	7,595
Gross margin (£)	**1,235**	**3,431**	**1,668**	**8,155**

a	Yields strongly influenced by seasonal factors
b	Also influenced by seasonal factors
c	Casual labour at £3.00/hr
d	Includes canes - four year life, annual cost £380
e	Includes £96 for vacuum clooling

FIELD VEGETABLES 2: FINANCIAL INFORMATION

General Information

Enterprise Item	Carrots	Onions	Lettuce	Leeks
Production & Marketing				
Total UK hectares	17,880	7,699	8,134	3,433
Estimated producer numbers	n/a	n/a	100-200	
Average unit size (ha)	15 - 100		5-45	
Average yield	depends on crop		depends on crop	
Marketing channels	Grower Co-operatives. Large independent packhouses. Wholesale markets, supermarkets, processors, some direct sales via farm shops/PYO, with emphasis on processors.			
Investment Considerations			**e.g. lettuce**	
Typical investment (£ /ha)	20-30,000[a][b]		100,000[c]	
Minimum size of unit (ha)	20-40		40	
Lead time to 1st crop	months		weeks	
Production cycles thereafter	continuous		continuous	
Cycles per year	1		5	
Rotational details	soil borne diseases		soil borne diseases	

a   Root lifting equipment £25,000
b   Drying and storage equipment £60-70,000
c   Specialist cooling equipment (vacuum cooler) £65,000 harvest rigs and trailers £20,000 each

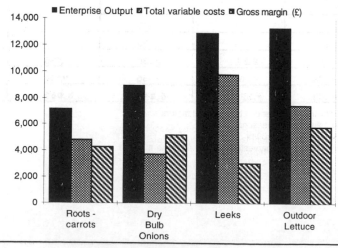

OUTSIDER'S GUIDE

SUMMARY

GROSS MARGINS

Enterprise Item	Roots - carrots	Dry Bulb Onions	Leeks	Outdoor Lettuce
Example variety	Nantes, Autumn King, Chantenay types	Rijnsburger F1 hybrids	e.g. Leeks according to season of marketing	Iceberg/crisphead types
OUTPUT				
Yield per Hectare (tonnes unless otherwise stated)[a]	45 (25 - 75)	50 tonnes (in 25 kg nets)	4,600 x 6.35 kg	3,700 x 12's
Price/unit of sale (£)[b]	160	180	2.80	3.60
Enterprise Output	**7,200**	**9,000**	**12,880**	**13,320**
VARIABLE COSTS (£) - Production				
Fertilisers	80	98	110	120
Sprays	260	118	132	225
Establishment seeds / bulbs / plants	175	910	475	1,200
Water	-	-	10	140
Sundries	-	-	-	-
Direct casual lab [c]	80	-	1,056	350
Subtotal production	**595**	**1,126**	**1,783**	**2,035**
VARIABLE COSTS (£) - Marketing				
Packing & cooling	1,200	400	1,472	1,998
Transport & handling	200	580	2,576	1,110
Harvesting packing - casual labour[c]	150[d]	300	2,700	990
Commission	720	900	1,288	1,332
Drying and storage	-	450	-	-
Sub total marketing	2,270	2,630	8,036	5,430
Total variable costs	4,865	3,756	9,819	7,465
Gross margin (£)	**4,335**	**5,244**	**3,061**	**5,855**

a   Yields strongly influenced by seasonal factors
b   Also influenced by seasonal factors
c   Casual labour at £3.00/hr
d   Involves specialist harvesting & lifting equipment

SPECIALIST SECTORS

D: PROTECTED VEGETABLES

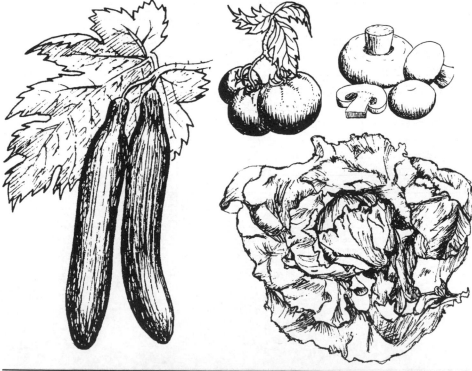

CUCUMBERS

PROTECTED VEGETABLES

Introduction

The section continues with those vegetables that are predominantly grown under controlled environmental conditions. You will note that those vegetables grown both in the field and under protection are covered in both Vegetable sections.

CUCUMBERS

An ancient tropical crop originating in Asia and known to have been grown on the Indian sub-continent for 3,000 years, cucumbers are thought to have been introduced into the UK in the 16th Century and grown only by the rich until development of glass houses allowed for wider production.

In much the same way as tomatoes, cucumbers are now produced in hi-tech glasshouse systems. Modern production uses computerised systems of control, mainly in soil-less systems.

A major step forward in cucumber production was the development of all female plants which reduced the time and the skill needed for production. Much of the UK production is centred in Humberside, with the bulk of production going to the supermarket outlets. Cucumber production is a high investment business requiring glass and computerised systems of production.

Availability from UK Producers

Jan	Feb	Mar	Apr	May	Jun	Jul	Aug	Sept	Oct	Nov	Dec
	▓	▓	▓	▓	▓	▓	▓	▓	▓		

Availability from Overseas Producers

	Jan	Feb	Mar	Apr	May	Jun	Jul	Aug	Sept	Oct	Nov	Dec
Netherlands	▓	▓	▓	▓	▓	▓	▓	▓	▓	▓	▓	
Spain	▓	▓								▓	▓	▓
Canary Islands	▓	▓								▓	▓	▓

CUCUMBERS

Key Facts

Area Grown (ha)	280
Gross Production ('000t)	117.7
UK Market Size ('000t)	176.21
UK Market Share (%)	63.70
UK Exports ('000t)	0.70
UK Imports ('000t)	64.01

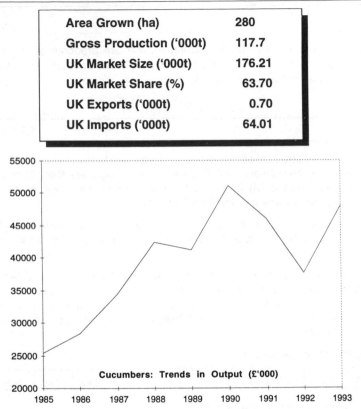

Cucumbers: Trends in Output (£'000)

Grading Standards

4 Classes : Extra, I, II and III

Sizing : determined by weight; Open : > 180g. Protected >250g.

Extra Class and Class I protected weighing:
 > 500 g = > 30cm length; 250g to 500g = >25cm length
Sizing is compulsory for Extra and Class I
The difference in weight between heaviest & lightest in package must not exceed:
100 g for range 180g to 400g and 150g for over 400 g

OUTSIDER'S GUIDE

Husbandry Summary

Varieties   Rebella, Corona, Pyralis, Bronco, Jessica

Soils   Rockwool slabs (90cm x 30cm x 7.5cm thick) at standard densities (700/0.1ha)

Environment Temperature: For Jan planted 20-21°C night, 21-23°C day. Gradual reduction to 17°C night and 19°C day in 0.25°C stages. Irrigation requirements: 1150 x 1000 litres per 0.1ha applied as required through automatic drip lines. Coal (60 tonnes/0.1ha) or heavy oil used. Carbon dioxide enrichment to 1000 vpm when vents closed. Use propane, paraffin. If pure CO_2 used maintain 335 vpm when vents open until June.

Training   Dutch cordon system used: alternate plants taken to overhead wires approx. 60cm apart. Fix thermal screens into place up to 6 weeks after planting. A later crop (with reduced heating costs) can be grown on straw bales over border soil, planting out in early-mid March. Yield/ha is lower.

Nutrition   Blueprint nutritional programmes used. Automatic systems such as VOCOM contol conductivitiy and pH. Fertigation used via drip lines to apply major elements, applying approx. 0.5 litres/plant/application.   Solar radiation figures and 150% of 'theoretical' used.

Production Cycle

Nov - Dec   Prepare production area, lay floor covering, stand out rockwool blocks.

Late Jan   Plant out block raised plants at 45cm spacing, approx. 14,000 plants/ha. Enrich with CO_2 and maintain blueprint temperature regimes. Introduce predators for the biological control of Red Spider Mite (Phytoseilus) and White Fly (Encarsia or Macrolophus). Routine sprays against other pests and diseases. Western Flower Thrip can be a problem (Amblyseius used).

Feb - Oct   Harvest crop into 6.0kg trays with strict quality control. Supermarket sales via marketing groups. Product shrink wrapped. 75-95% Class 1 grade out possible.

B'HEAD LETTUCE

BUTTERHEAD LETTUCE

Lettuce is an ancient vegetable, believed to have been introduced into Britain by the Romans. It has been recommended for its medicinal and herbal properties throughout the centuries.

During the last decade tremendous changes have been experienced in salad vegetables. Demand has increased considerably and UK producers have risen to meet the challenge of year round availability from imported produce.

About 60% of Round or Butterhead lettuce is grown in glasshouses or polytunnels in order to achieve year-round British lettuce supplies. Some round lettuce is grown outside in traditional market-garden areas during favourable weather conditions. Most outdoor crops are raised from seed sown in peat blocks or cell trays under glass and transplanted while the plants are small. Lettuce is highly susceptible to disease so constant research is being carried out to breed disease-resistant varieties. Light conditions affect growth so winter grown lettuces tend to weigh less than summer ones.

Availability from UK Producers

Jan	Feb	Mar	Apr	May	Jul	Jul	Aug	Sept	Oct	Nov	Dec

Availability from Overseas Producers (Butterhead)

	Jan	Feb	Mar	Apr	May	Jul	Jul	Aug	Sept	Oct	Nov	Dec
France												
Netherlands												

Key Facts:

	Field	Protected
Area Grown (ha)	6,881	1,221
Gross Production ('000t)	201.40	46.50
UK Market Size ('000t)		296.50
UK Market Share (%)		68.80
UK Exports ('000t)		1.70
UK Imports ('000t)		92.60

B'HEAD LETTUCE

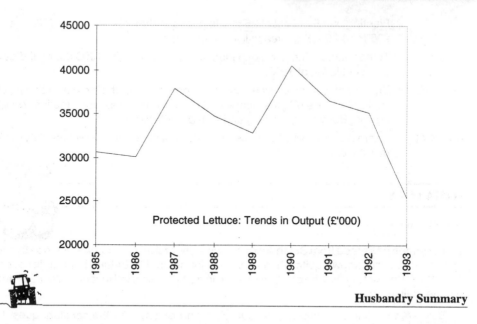

Protected Lettuce: Trends in Output (£'000)

Husbandry Summary

Varieties	Butterhead types - refer to latest seed house catalogues e.g. Rachel, Kira, Lianne.
Soils	Border soil, soil sterilisation biennially (Methyl bromide).
Environment	Temperature regimes: 2°C minimum night, 4°C minimum day. Ventilate crop at 10-20°C depending on season, and carbon dioxide use. Heating systems required to maintain minimum temps.
	Irrigation requirements: 700 x 1000 litres per 0.1ha applied as required through automatic drip lines.
	Heating oil (3500 sec) to maintain above temps. 5 x 1000 litres.
	Carbon dioxide enrichment to 1000 vpm from March - November in bright light conditions. Use propane, paraffin or pure carbon dioxide.
Nutrition	Base dressings in border soil (per 0.1 hectare)
	35kg Sulphate of potash, 35kg Keiserite, 50kg Nitroform, 100kg Nitrochalk per hectare.

Production Cycle

Year Round	For successional supplies of block plants split pil seed is sown in 3.8cm blocks in a proprietary compost e.g. for September planting, sow in August. Artificial lighting will be required at certain times of the year. Minimum temperature for germination 15°C (10° - 18°C acceptable).

TOMATOES

Planting out: Plant out at 25 plants per sq.m throughout season (200 mm x 200 mm) 90 - 95% area utilisation possible.

Temperatures during propagation stage: 6°C at night, 10°C during the day with ventilation at 18°C.

Jan - Feb   Enrich with carbon dioxide. Introduce predators for the biological control of Red Spider Mite (Phytoseilus) and White Fly (Macrolophus). Routine sprays against Botrytis (Iprodione) and Aphids (Pirimicarb).

Mar - Oct   Harvest crop into 4.5 kg boxes with strict quality control. May/June/July peak months of production.

TOMATOES

Introduction

Tomatoes originated from South America and were probably brought to Europe by the Spaniards. It is not known quite when they were introduced to Britain, but the discovery during the 19th century that the plants flourished in glasshouses, led to rapid cultivation and commercialisation.

Research continues to improve flavour, yield and quality with the constant quest to breed new varieties. UK growers are sponsoring research and development through the Horticultural Development Council.

Nearly all tomatoes grown in the UK are produced under glass, just a few outdoor tomatoes are grown for PYO outlets. About 80% of the crop is grown in heated glasshouses under very controlled conditions, while the remainder is produced during the normal season in 'cold' houses.

Availability from UK Producers

Jan	Feb	Mar	Apr	May	Jun	Jul	Aug	Sept	Oct	Nov	Dec
		░	░	░	░	░	░	░	░		

Availability From Overseas Producers

	Jan	Feb	Mar	Apr	May	Jun	Jul	Aug	Sept	Oct	Nov	Dec
Canary Islands	░	░	░							░	░	░
Netherlands	░	░	░	░	░	░	░	░	░	░	░	
Spain	░	░	░							░	░	░

TOMATOES

Area Grown ha)	473
Gross Production ('000t)	133.7
UK Market Size ('000t)	357.2
UK Market Share (%)	26.3
UK Exports ('000t)	37.8
UK Imports ('000t)	263.2

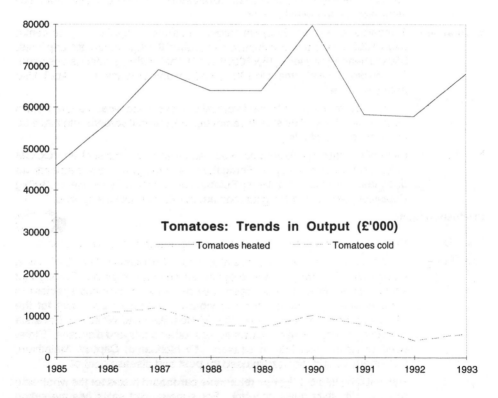

Tomatoes: Trends in Output (£'000)

——— Tomatoes heated   ········ Tomatoes cold

Grading Standards

4 classes: Extra I, II, III

Sizing: Based on diameter, but not for cherry tomatoes.

TOMATOES

Minimum Size:

Class Extra, I, and II: Round and ribbed: 35 mm; Oblong: 30mm

(Extra and Class I observe compulsory sliding scale)
Class III: Oblong & All Protected tomatoes: 20 mm diameter
Others: 35mm Class III

Husbandry Summary

Varieties   Liberto, Calypso, Vanessa, Blizzard, Counter, Guindilla. Unheated varieties: Goldstar, Turbo.

Soils   Recyclable high density Rockwool slabs (90 cm x 30cm x 7.5cm thick) at standard densities (1250/0.1ha). Unheated crop: border soil, after soil sterilisation with Methyl bromide.

Environment   Temperature regimes: Blueprint programmes used. Irrigation requirements: 570 x 1000 litres per 0.1ha applied as required through automatic drip lines. 960sec heating oil used. (45 x 1000 litres/0.1ha). Other grades can be used. Carbon dioxide enrichment to 1000 vpm from dawn to sunset until April. Use propane, paraffin.

Training system: Plants trained vertically to overhead wire. Layered down as plant develops. Side shoots removed. Fix thermal screens into place up to 6 weeks after planting.

Nutrition   Blueprint nutrition programmes used. Automatic systems such as VOCOM control conductivity and pH. Fertigation used to apply major elements via drip lines. Unheated crop: 190kg Sulphate of potash, 127kg Keiserite, 300kg Potassium nitrate and 90kg ammonium nitrate per hectare applied.

Production Cycle

Nov - Dec   Prepare production area, lay floor covering, stand out rockwool blocks.

Jan - Feb   Plant out plants in rockwool cubes at approx. 2750 plants/0.1ha. Enrich with carbon dioxide and maintain blueprint temperature regimes. Throughout season when flower trusses open, use bee inserts (Bombus species) to cross pollinate, or use electric bee vibrator. Introduce predators for the biological control of Red Spider Mite (Phytoseilus) and White Fly (Encarsia or Macrolophus). Routine sprays against other pests and diseases. Ethrel used to ripen fruits late in season. Dichlofluanid, Captan, Malathion, Deltamethrin, and Vinclozolin used for pest and disease control.

Apr - Oct   Harvest crop into 5.44kg non returnable cardboard boxes for the wholesale market, with strict quality control. For supermarket sales (via marketing groups) crop harvested into plastic crates, taken to grader to be sized, colour graded and pre-packed. Modern equipment highly automated. Cool chain distribution necessary (5-8°C).

MUSHROOMS

MUSHROOMS

Mushrooms represent a specialist crop across Europe. The edible mushroom is not a higher plant but a fungus - Agaricus bisporus - and because of this its life cycle is completely different to other horticultural crops.

The earliest known record of mushroom cultivation relates to French production in 1650.

The cultivation is by minute spores shed from the undersides of the mushroom. From these spores grow tiny mycelium (a laboratory technique) which are impregnated into cereal grains known as 'spawn'. These are mixed with specially prepared compost which results in rapid colonisation or 'running'.

The surface is then 'capped' with peat and lime and three weeks later mushrooms can be picked. The crop is over within six weeks with the strongest flushes occurring in the first three.

One of the major problems to be overcome in mushroom production is occurring control of Sciarid fly. HRI Littlehampton is researching biological control methods which when developed could have far reaching consequences, not only for mushroom growers but for horticulture in general.

Much work is being carried out to find alternatives to bisporus - a UK native. There are over 40 wild Agarici native to the UK and great potential exists in developing these for commercial production.

Availability from UK Producers

Jan	Feb	Mar	Apr	May	Jun	Jul	Aug	Sept	Oct	Nov	Dec
▪	▪	▪	▪	▪	▪	▪	▪	▪	▪	▪	▪

Availability from Overseas Producers

	Jan	Feb	Mar	Apr	May	Jun	Jul	Aug	Sept	Oct	Nov	Dec
Irish Republic	▪	▪	▪	▪	▪	▪	▪	▪	▪	▪	▪	▪
Netherlands	▪	▪	▪	▪	▪	▪	▪	▪	▪	▪	▪	▪
Belgium / Lux.	▪	▪	▪	▪	▪	▪	▪	▪	▪	▪	▪	▪

Key Facts

Area Grown (ha)	431
Gross Production ('000t)	118.60
UK Market Size ('000t)	154.03
UK Market Share (%)	76.20
UK Exports ('000t)	1.35
UK Imports ('000t)	36.58

MUSHROOMS

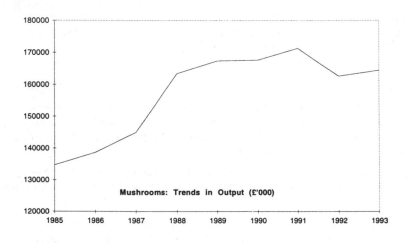

Mushrooms: Trends in Output (£'000)

Grading Standards
None available.

Husbandry Summary

Varieties   Agaricus bisporus. Shiitake and Oyster mushrooms also grown.

Medium   Compost from straw, horse little, poultry manure. Initially it is composted by mixing and turning , adding water regularly over 7-10 days, reaching temperatures of 76°C killing most pests and pathogens. Second phase involves 'peak heating' (pasteurisation) often called ("sweat out") at 60°C. This is used to fill troughs, trays, shelves and conditioned at 52°C.

Environment   Traditionally grown in Lea Valley insulated plastic tunnels or in purpose-build block-walled building. Crop requires total darkness with water, and a heating system (steam-injected hot water) to maintain growing environment year round. Mushrooms grown in troughs 0.9 x 1.2m x 15-23cm deep, stacked 4-5 high inside the buildings. A recent trend is to grow in 28kg polythene bags (0.1-0.2m²).

Nutrition   Derived entirely from compost.

Production Cycle

Spawning   On final turning of composed it is 'spawned' by incorporating the spawn at 0.5% by weight. Spawn is cultured on sterilised rye or millet grain for ease of handling.

Growing   After stacking in buildings, temperature maintained at 24°C at 2% carbon dioxide. Troughs 'cased' with a peat/limestone topping 3.8-5.0cm thick and of neutral pH. The spawn will 'run' through the containers in about two weeks.

Air temperature then reduce to 16-18°C and Carbon dioxide reduced to 600-1000ppm. after 3 weeks first mushrooms appear. These are cut, and 4-5 'flushes' will appear at weekly intervals. 5-6 crops can be taken from each growing room before quality and size deteriorates.

Harvesting   By hand and the traditional mushroom 'chip' is widely used. Buttons and flats are cut with a short stem, varying according to customer and requirement. Supermarkets require their own containers and specifications. Cool chain distribution (3°C) is essential.

Health   As the crop is grown in sterile conditions, it is vulnerable to attack - Diptera sp. are the worst - Sciarids, Cecids and Phorids. Other pests include Tarsonemid mites and Nematodes. MV's (viruses) and Verticillium Wilt (dry bubble), pathogenic bacteria (Brown Blotch, Mummy disease and Drippy Gill) are a problem. Parasitic fungi (False Truffle, Wet Bubble, Cobweb Fungus - Dactylium-) are also troublesome. Rigorous hygiene must be maintained at all times. Methyle bromide fumigation can be employed using registered contractors.

SUMMARY

FINANCIAL INFORMATION

Enterprise Item	Tomatoes Heated	Tomatoes Unheated	Lettuce	Cucumbers	Mushrooms
Production & Marketing					
Total UK hectares[b]	400	155	1,440[a]	230	431
Estimated producer numbers	50 - 100	85 - 125	150 - 200	50 - 75	<300[c]
Average unit size (ha)	1.3	0.5 - 2.5	0.5 - 1.5	1 - 3	0.5 - 1.0
Average yield t/ha	240 - 300	100 - 125	31	389	202
Marketing channels	Supermarkets via grower packhouses / co-operatives; wholesale markets / secondary markets; some processors				
Investment Considerations					
Typical investment (£ /m²)	20 - 55[e]	20 - 55	20 - 55 or 10 - 15	20 - 55 or 10 - 15	18-20[e]
Minimum size of unit (ha)	0.5	0.5	0.1	0.1-0.5	0.5
Lead time to first crop	4 - 5 mths	4 - 5 mths	6 - 8 weeks	1 - 2 mths	3-4 weeks
Production cycles thereafter	Annual	Annual	Continuous	Continuous	4-5
Cycles per year	1	1	7	1	5-6
Rotational details	none with substrate growing	none with substrate growing	Soil sterilisation necessary	Soil sterilisation	none

a   Cropped area used continuously throughout the year (up to 7 cycles)
b   Total protected vegetable area is about 2,700 - 3000 hectares (allowing for multiple cropping practices from 1 hectare).
c   There are three large producers, including Linfield Middlebrook. The Mushroom Growers' Association is very important to the industry.
d   122,000 tonnes produced annually valued at £165 million at market and £700 million at retail.
e   Typical investment costs are shown below:

Glasshouses	Venlo glasshouses range from £20 - 25/square metre for 4,000m² and over, to £40/m² for 1,000 to 2,000m². Wide span glasshouses are £25 - 35/m². Polytunnels (4.26m x 36.6m) cost £10-15/m² while multi-span tunnels cost £12-16/m².
Heating systems	Boilers with 1,500 kw output range from £12,000 - £35,000 depending on the fuel type used (gas, coal, oil/gas). Pipe systems cost £50,000 - £100,000 depending on self-installation or contractor installation. Air heaters with 800,000 BTU's/hour cost about £5,000 - £6,500.
Other investments	Thermal screening: £14,000 - £26,000/ hectare. Nutrient film technique (for substrate growing) £18,000 - £40,000/hectare. Computers for environmental control are about £2,500 per compartment. Graders: £15,000 - 1000,000 each depending on volume and sophistication. Mushroom composting machine costs £20,000 - 30,000. Refridgeration £20,000.

SUMMARY

GROSS MARGINS

Item	Enterprise Tomatoes Heated	Lettuce	Cucumbers	Mushrooms Figures estimated from J. Nix
Example variety	Calypso, Liberto, Daniella, Morocco	Butterhead types	Jessica, Korona	Agaricus bisporous, Shiitake, Oyster forms.
OUTPUT				
Yield per hectare (tonnes per **0.1 ha**)	37 6,700x 5.45 kg	1,600 x 12's (7 crops)	54 9,000 x 6 kg	48
Price/unit of sale (£)	4.20[a]	2.20	3.20	1.25/kg
Enterprise output	**28,140**	**24,640**	**28,800**	**120,000**
VARIABLE COSTS - Production				
Fertilisers	610	75	880	6,000
Sprays[b]	285	120	510	1,000
Establishment seeds / bulbs / plants	950	1,650	1,350	14,000
Fuel[c]	7,200	510	3,200	9,000
Water[d]	240	175	295	
Sundries (incl. rockwool & bees)	1,850	235	1,350	1,000
Subtotal production (£)	**11,135**	**2,765**	**7,585**	**31,000**
VARIABLE COSTS (£) - Marketing				
Packaging	1,809	2,800	2,360	2,500
Transport & handling	1,675	2,800	4,320	3,500
Harvest, labour/packing[e]	1,503	2,700	1,755	50,000
Commission (10%)	2,814	2,464	2,880	12,000
Subtotal marketing (£)	**7,801**	**10,764**	**11,315**	**68,000**
Total variable costs	18,936	13,529	18,900	99,000
Gross margin / 0.1 ha	**9,204**	**11,111**	**9,900**	**21,000**

a   Sensitive to imports (from Holland) and seasonal effects including 'back garden' crops.
b   Includes biological control.
c   Includes carbon dioxide enrichment and electricity.
d   Plants grown in rockwool blocks on polythene - 'substrate' culture. Bees for pollination.
e   Casual labour at $3.00/hr for harvesting and packing.

Note: All figures are for 0.1 hectare.
Mushroom growing is not recommended as a casual enterprise as expertise is required in environment and disease control.

GROSS MARGINS

Gross Margins

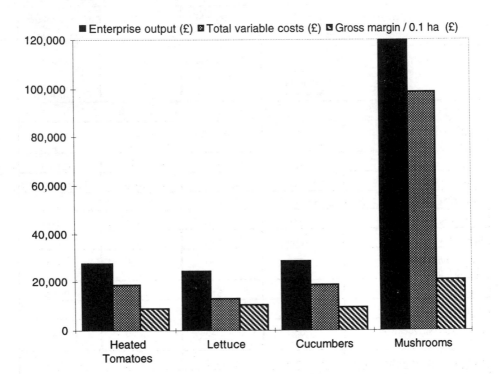

EXOTICS

The range of produce available to the UK consumer continues to grow. Improved transport systems mean that exotic fruit and vegetables can now be delivered to UK outlets from all corners of the globe.

As consumer tastes change, the demand from outlets is high. The majority of these crops are imported despite the fact that many could be grown successfully here in the UK. Traditionalists may see these crops as only a passing phase, however, the potato was an exotic vegetable in its day. The sale of exotic fruit and vegetables is already big business in the UK and continues to grow.

One company importing exotic farm produce already handles 65 lines from 55 countries, totalling 70 tons of air-freighted produce daily into its Heathrow warehouse. Many of these exotic crops will never be economically grown in the UK but some are commercially viable.

Increased UK production of the following crops would help to reduce the cost of :

1 Globe Artichokes

95% of the home market is imported from France.

2 Courgettes

UK production could be doubled, strong processing market, medium for retail and a market for small immature fruits for the restaurant market.

3 Fennel

Entire crop currently imported from France and Italy.

4 Kohl Rabi

Twice the UK production is imported.

5 Chillies

Grow well in the UK under polythene.

6 Mangetout peas

Entire crop currently imported.

7 Squashes

Good demand for vegetarian spaghetti and Pattypan Squashes.

8 Coriander

This grows readily under field conditions and provides continuous supplies of the fresh leaved product from May through to the Autumn to meet a rising interest in foreign dishes and flavours.

EXOTICS

9 Sweet Peppers

Increased demand could be met by UK rockwool slab production under specific growing regime throughout summer months.

10 Aubergines

60% imported from Holland, 25% from Spain. Recent increase in popularity in Britain could be met by home-production under glass.

Others include:-

Beans, herbs, horseradish and particularly baby vegetables including carrots, leeks, cauliflowers, cabbage. A strong UK demand exists especially from the restaurant market with demand currently being met by imports.

SPECIALIST SECTORS

E: FIELD GROWN FLOWERS & BULBS

NOTES

INTRODUCTION

FIELD GROWN FLOWERS & BULBS

Traditional field flower and bulb growing continues in those areas suited to such production e.g. the Spalding area in Linclolnshire and the sheltered parts of Cornwall and the Isles of Scilly.

The area occupied by field grown flowers and bulbs is about 6,000 hectares.

Narcissi (daffodils) are by far the UK's most important crop, occupying 4048 hectares. The UK is amongst the worlds largest producers of daffodils. Tulips have declined as a bulb crop.

Approximately half the output is retained for re-planting, 75% of the remainder is marketed as dry bulbs, mostly through Garden Centres, DIY stores and mail order. 25% of the output is forced for flower production.

Lincolnshire grows nearly 65% of the UK's bulbs. Cornwall and the Isles of Scilly are the main flower producing areas.

Bulb exportation has been a rare success story for horticulture, despite high imports from the well organised Dutch bulb industry (mostly tulips and hyacinths). Many large growers, exporters, importers and packers are based in the Spalding area (e.g. Geest and Lingarden).

Other outdoor flower crops include chrysanthemums, roses, dahlias, gladioli, irises and anemones. All have seen a resurgence of consumer demand in recent years.

Roses and dahlias remain a favourite Garden Centre and pre-packed plant line for DIY stores. Most cut flowers are marketed through the wholesale markets or via van sales. Small areas of hardy annuals are grown for the cut flower trade, and there is a thriving, specialist dried flower industry. The principle customers are the floristry trade, especially Interflora and Garden Centres.

The main field crops that will be considered in this Guide are Narcissi, Tulips and Gladioli.

NARCISSUS (DAFFODIL)

Narcissus is the botanical name for all the different varieties of daffodil of which there are over 1,000. These are commonly listed by specialist firms, ranging from tiny miniatures only 5cm high to mighty trumpet daffodils with flowers 15cm across on stems 50cm high. The varieties are grouped into 11 divisions e.g. Div. 2: large-cupped, Div. 3: small-cupped, Div. 4: double and Div. 10: wild.

Narcissi can be used for forcing, bedding, cutting and naturalising. Flowers can be available from Christmas to the end of May, depending on varieties and methods of cultivation.

NARCISSI

Narcissi commercially grown for the cut flower market are best replanted every second or third year. The first year after planting is regarded as an establishment period as the blooms and numbers of them are unlikely to be optimum. The second year produces the very best flowers.

Most of the early-season flower production is in the South West where the climate is milder and the price higher during the winter. As daffodils become generally more plentiful during the spring the price drops and growers in Lincolnshire, the other important production area, may tend to specialise in bulb production, the flowers only being a secondary product of their enterprise.

Trends

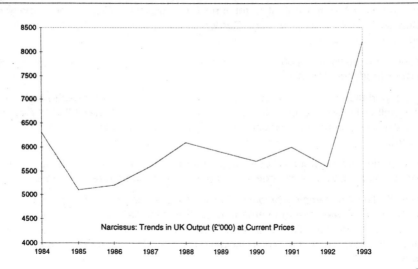

Narcissus: Trends in UK Output (£'000) at Current Prices

Husbandry Summary

Varieties	Golden Harvest, Carlton, from ordinary commercial stock. Also: Cheerfulness, Hollywood, Dutch Master. Other varieties include: Fortune, White Lion, Ice Follies, Unsurpassable. A range of varieties may be grown for cut flower market, less for bulb production.
Soils	Fine sandy loams of Class 1 grade. Stone free silts ideal. Level, well drained sites preferred. Land occupied for 3 growing seasons.
Nutrition	Following soil analysis and dressings to bring fertility up to indices 3, annual applications of 80kg N, 130kg P and 300kg K per hectareare recommended.

OUTSIDER'S GUIDE

Production Cycle

Following autumn/winter ploughing, cultivate in spring and ridge field in May/June.

July - Aug   Plant out at 15 tonnes/ha. Bulb population approx. 270,000 bulbs/ha using 11-13cm grade. Ridges set out at 76cm. Bulbs scattered in 20-25cm bands. Stock bulbs planted at about 1.14kg/metre of ridge. Each hectare has about 13,000m of ridge.

Linuron, Diquat/Paraquat, Lenacil and Cyanazine herbicides used pre and post planting. Irrigation may be necessary to establish the crop. Provision to apply 80-100mm should be made. Raingun application acceptable.

Crop protection programme : Benomyl and Mancozeb fungicides used.

Aug - Sept   Plant for bulb production mainly (and flower crop taken in 2nd year). Bulbs are given Hot Water Treatment (HWT) against Basal Rot. Thiabendazol added to tank mix. It can also be used as a post lifting spray. For Dec/Jan flowering, prepared bulbs used. These are subjected to artificial temperature conditions to change the natural season. Income up on value of flower crop, but bulb yield severely reduced.

Feb - Mar   Flower crop harvested. Year 1: 15,000 stems/tonne planted average. Year 2: 35,000 stems/tonne planted average. 10 stems/bunch, 50 bunches/cardboard outer. Yield 500 - 500,000 stems/ha.

Jun - Jul   Bulbs lifted with undercutter, wind-rowed to dry, carted to drying room and storage. Average bulb increase 100%. Size grades 12-14cm and 14-16cm. 15 tonnes/ha yield. Same tonnage (<12cm>16cm) retained as stock for planting. Remainder sold off as bulbs.

TULIPS

Tulips were originally brought from Turkey to Holland over 300 years ago where the Dutch bulb industry began. Competition in the UK market from Holland is strong but there are still a significant number of tulip producers around Spalding, Lincolnshire, where the fenlands provide ideal rich soil conditions. Growers mostly concentrate on bulb production but flowers are also grown and sold to the cut-flower market if economically viable.

Tulips, like Narcissi, come in a range of sizes from miniatures to tall, elegant blooms. Some are cup-shaped, some frilled, some open star-shaped in the sun, some are single blooms and others multi-headed. The range of colours are vast from white, through yellows, oranges, reds and mauves, some pure colours and other striped or mottled. Tulip bulbs multiply after planting in the Autumn ready for lifting the following season.

TULIPS

Trends

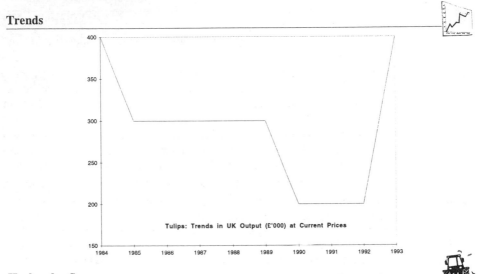

Tulips: Trends in UK Output (£'000) at Current Prices

Husbandry Summary

Varieties
Apeldoorn and Darwin hybrids. A range of varieties may be grown for cut flower market, less for bulb production.

Soils
Fine sandy loams of Class 1 grade. Stone free silts ideal. Level, well drained sites preferred.

Nutrition
Following soil analysis and dressings to bring fertility up to indices 3, annual applications of 100kg N, 100kg P and 200kg K per hectare are recommended.

Production Cycle

Following autumn/winter ploughing, cultivate in spring and ridge field in May/June.

Sept - Oct
Plant out at 4-6 tonnes/ha. Ridges set out at 70-74cm. Bulbs scattered in 20-25cm bands. Stock bulbs planted at about 1.25kg/metre of ridge. Each hectare has about 15,000m of ridge. Paraquat, Lenacil and Cyanazine herbicides used pre and post planting. Irrigation may be necessary to establish the crop. Provision to apply 80-100mm should be made. Raingun application acceptable. Crop Protection Programme: Benomyl and Mancozeb fungicides used.

Mar - Apr
Flower crop harvested. 5 stems/bunch, 100,000 bunches/ha. Marketed in non-returnable cardboard boxes.

July
Bulbs lifted with undercutter, wind-rowed to dry, carted to drying room and storage. Average bulb increase 100-150%. 6-8 tonne/ha yield. 4-6 tonnes/ha retained as stock for planting.

GLADIOLI

GLADIOLI

These tall, stately flowers fall into four main categories: large-flowered, primulinus hybrids, butterflies and miniatures. The large flowered varieties have always been the most popular, the other three types being somewhat smaller, often with ruffled or frilled florets, and striking petal markings.

Gladioli come in a superb range of colours and if planted in succession, offer a continuous supply of blooms throughout the summer. Gladioli are grown from corms, which must be planted sufficiently deep (15cm minimum) in soil to prevent the tall heavy stems from collapsing.

Trends

No figures available.

Husbandry Summary

Varieties	A range of varieties may be grown for cut flower market to give continuity of cutting. Ordinary commercial stock used.
Soils	Fine sandy loams of Class 1 grade. Stone free silts ideal. Level, well drained sites preferred.
Nutrition	Following soil analysis and dressings to bring fertility up to indices 3, annual applications of 90kg N, 75kg P and 175kg K per hectare are recommended.

Production Cycle

Following autumn/winter ploughing, cultivate in spring and ridge field in May/June.

Mar - May   Plant out at 250,000 corms per hectare (8-10cm grade). 20cm bands of corms planted in ridges 70cm -75cm apart. Paraquat and Lenacil herbicides used pre and post planting. Irrigation may be necessary to establish the crop. Provision to apply 80-100mm should be made. Raingun application acceptable. Some roguing carried out. Crop protection programme: Benomyl and Malathion pesticides used.

Aug - Sept   Flower crop harvested. 5 stems/bunch, 220,000 bunches/ha. Marketed in non-returnable cardboard boxes, 2200 boxes/ha, 20 x 5 bunches/box.

Sept - Oct   Corms lifted with undercutter, wind-rowed to dry, cleaned and carted to store. Average corm retrieval 60-65% (150,000+ per ha) of mixed sizes. 150,000 corms/ha retained as stock for planting.

SUMMARY

FINANCIAL INFORMATION

Crop Item	FLOWERS			BULBS	
	Narcissi Year 1	Narcissi Year 2	Gladioli	Tulips	Narcissi
Production & Marketing					
Hectares	4048 total[b]	4048 total[b]	140	158	4048 total[b]
Number of Producers	n/a	n/a	n/a	n/a	n/a
Av. Unit Size (approx.)	4 - 40	4 - 40	13	13	4 - 40
Average Yield tonnes/ha (unless otherwise stated)	15,000 stems /tonne planted	30-35,000 stems/t planted	220,000 x 5 stems (2200 boxes)	6.5 - 7.0	15 - 20
Marketing Channels	Primary/ secondary wholesalers, Direct retail outlets, Ex -nursery from packhouse door, Van sales, Mail order, Garden & plant centres, Local Authorities, some Supermarket sales.				
Investment Considerations					
Typical investment (£ /ha)	900[a]		900[a]	900[a]	900[a]
Minimum size of Unit (ha)	13-14		13-14	13-14	13-14
Lead time to first crop (yrs)	1		1	1	1
Production cycles thereafter	2		-	1	2
Cycles per year	1		1	1	1
Rotational details	-		-	-	-

a   This assumes the land is rented. Items include normal requirements for an intensive arable farm under 100 ha. For land purchase add £5,000 per hectare.

b   No breakdown figures available for flower / bulb production split.

SUMMARY

GROSS MARGINS

Enterprise Item	FLOWERS			BULBS	
	Narcissi Year 1	Narcissi Year 2	Gladioli	Tulips	Narcissi
Example variety	Golden Harvest; Carlton; Cheerfulness		Various	Apeldoorn; Darwin hybrids	Golden Harvest; Carlton
OUTPUT					
Yield per hectare (tonnes unless otherwise stated)	15,000 stems /tonne planted	30-35,000 stems/ tonne planted (1100 boxes/ha)[a]	220,000 stems (2200 boxes)	6.5 - 7.0 sold 4 retained	15 - 20 sold 15 retained
Price/unit of sale (£)	9.25 per box	9.25 per box	6.25	820/t	375/t
Enterprise output (£/ha)	**4,162**	**10,175** **10,275**[b]	**13,750** **2,500**[c]	**5,330** **1,800**[d]	**6,562** **4,500**[e]
VARIABLE COSTS (£) - Production					
Fertilisers	110	-	80	100	100
Sprays	140	150	150	70	245
Establishment seeds / bulbs / plants	4,875	-	4,000	1,800	4,500
Sundries	600	-	-	-	500
Direct casual labour	510	390	1716	1452	800
Subtotal production (£)	**6,235**	**540**	**5,946**	**3,422**	**6,145**
VARIABLE COSTS (£) - Marketing					
Casual labour grading packing[f]	1,014	1,797	1,800	2,400	774
Packaging	225	650	946	50	100
Commission and handling (13%)	541	1,322	1,787	-	-
Transport	405	1,250	1,430	-	-
Subtotal marketing (£)	2,185	5,019	5,963	2,450	874
Enter output (£ / hectare)	**4,612**	**20,450**	**15,250**	**7,130**	**11,062**
Total variable costs	8,420	5,559	11,909	5,872	7,019
Gross margin (£/ha)	**5,316 per annum** **(averaged over 2 years)**		**4,341**	**1,258**	**4,043**

a 1 box x 50 bunches. 1 bunch = 50 stems
b 600 nets of bulbs @ £9.00/net. 15 tonnes @ £325/tonne retained as planting stock
c 60-65% retrieval of corms @ £400/t for replanting stock
d 4 tonnes @ £450/tonne retained as planting stock
e 15 tonnes @ £300/tonne retained as planting stock
f charged at £3.00 per hour where allocated

SUMMARY

Gross Margin

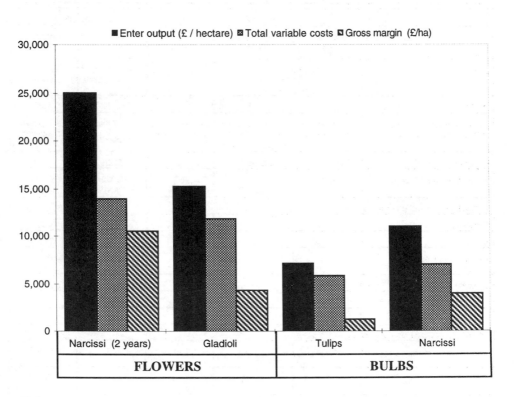

■ Enter output (£ / hectare) ▨ Total variable costs ◩ Gross margin (£/ha)

	FLOWERS		BULBS	
	Narcissi (2 years)	Gladioli	Tulips	Narcissi

Note:
The Narcissi enterprise runs for a two year cycle. The chart shows the output, the variable costs and the gross margin for those two years. To compare the enterprise with the other flower and bulb operations, divide the gross margin by 2 to give the annual averaged over the two years of the cycle.

SPECIALIST SECTORS

F: PROTECTED FLOWERS & PLANTS

NOTES

FLOWER CROPS GROWN UNDER PROTECTION

Chrysanthemums (68 hectares), Carnations (9 hectares), Alstroemerias, pot plants and bedding plants are the major crops grown. A small hectarage of cut roses remains and carnation hectarage has declined rapidly as a result of severe competition from countries like Israel and Colombia. Cut and pot chrysanthemums are available year round, and dominate the market.

The major growers are along the South Coast in East Sussex and Hampshire, together with growers in Essex, Lancashire and Yorkshire. The wholesale markets in the large conurbations remain significant outlets, but ex-nurseries supply the market. Co-operatives in this sector are rare.

Florists, street traders, garage forecourts and roadside sellers are the traditional outlets, together with some multiples. As a major outlet Marks and Spencer plc remains a market leader, particularly servicing the 'plant gift' market sector.

There has been a steady increase in the foliage and pot plant market, together with a number of specialist crops grown for particular seasons e.g. Poinsettias and Cyclamen for Christmas, all pot plants for Mother's Day and Easter. The growth of the conservatory market sector has increased sales of larger potted plants. Environmentally friendly offices and municipal buildings enhance working conditions with wide use of plant material.

All sectors face fierce competition from the Dutch, who have gained a greater market share in the past decade. This will not decrease with the continuing ease of cross -channel transport, and large volumes available from the Dutch Auction market system.

The English bedding plant industry, whether producing traditional 'trays', 'strips' or 'pots', has been an expanding market, with a 22 million tray and 90 million pot output. The introduction of brand leaders like "Colour packs" has revolutionised marketing, and developed a new range of instant, modular products, including vegetable and fruit plants. Garden and plant centres, together with roadside sellers, street traders and van sales, are the main outlets. Local authorities are also major users. The greater use of patio planters and hanging baskets have extended the range of material supplied (eg. Pansies, Polyanthus).

Details will now be given for the major flower crops grown : Cut Chrysanthemums, Pot Chrysanthemums and Carnations. 'Bedding plants' covers a vast range of flower varieties, but the basic seed-raising technique is generally applied. Foliage pot plants also includes a huge range of species and Poinsettias have been selected as a typical example of a specialist pot plant.

CHRYSANTHEMUMS

ALL YEAR ROUND CHRYSANTHEMUMS (CUT STEMS)

There are simply thousands of varieties of Chrysanthemum, in all colour shades and all bloom styles, some tight pompoms, some loose sprays and some with a contrasting centre.

Some Chrysanthemums are field grown but many are protected under glass. They are propagated either by root cuttings or by block raised plants from seed. Under natural conditions, Chrysanthemums planted in the Spring will flower as the daylength shortens from August through to November depending on variety. However, under protection and with the aid of artificial daylength by overhead blackout screening, and using controlled temperature conditions, Chrysanthemums can easily be encouraged to flower all the year round. Commercial producers obviously grow accordingly to meet the demand during the popular seasons for flowers e.g. Christmas, Mothering Sunday and Easter.

Trends

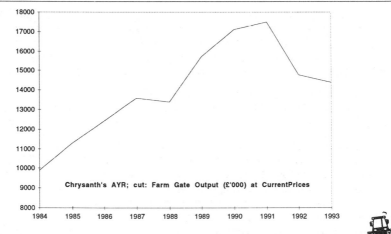

Chrysanth's AYR; cut: Farm Gate Output (£'000) at CurrentPrices

Husbandry Summary

Varieties	Huricane, Snowdon, Delta, Pink Gin, Rosado, Pasadoble, Blue Hawaii, Puma types.
Medium	Border soil, sterilised (sheet steam) yearly. Methyl bromide also used.
Environment	Blueprint schedules for temperature regimes (HRI Efford). Minimum day temperature 16°C. Ventilate at 18°C. . With carbon dioxide ventilate at 21°C. Night temperatures: 1st Wk March 17°C; 2nd Wk March 16°C; mid March to Oct 13°C; Nov 18°C; Dec to Jan19°C; Feb 18°C. 960 sec heating oil used. 27.5 x 1000 litres per 0.1ha to maintain temperature regimes.

Plant populations : 12.5cm X 12.5cm giving 189,630 plants/0.1ha. Winter populations reduced by 8-10%. 3.8 crop cycles per annum.

CARNATIONS

Nutrition	Base dressings of 171kg/0.1ha Triple superphosphate, 160kg/0.1 ha Ammonium nitrate, 380kg/0.1ha Sulphate of potash.

Production Cycle

Year Round	Depending on marketing strategy, which may require increased supplies at Christmas, Easter or Mothering Sunday Day, a proportion of the area is always being prepared and planted, whilst harvesting is carried out elsewhere. Rooted cuttings or block raised plants used. Blueprint schedules of daylengths depending on the time of year achieved by overhead blackout screening (also used as a thermal screen in winter for fuel economy - 55% saving). Artificial lighting used to increase daylength during periods of short daylight hours to maintain photoperiodic response for regular cropping.
Nov - Mar	Atmosphere enriched with carbon dioxide (paraffin source) at 1000 vpm.
	Irrigation and nutrition: Blue print nutritional programmes inject N P K and Mg into the irrigation lines.
Crop health	Biological control of the main pests is practised. Sticky cards also used for Aphid control. Predatory species are introduced into crop as pests (White Fly, Thrip, Spider Mite) build up. If unsuccessful approved compounds used (Aldicarb, Diazinon, Iprodione, Cypermethrin).
Harvesting	5 stems are hand cut and sleeved into a wrap. 20 wraps per box are marketed in non returnable cardboard boxes if transported to the wholesale market. Direct sales more important, often saving on packaging.

YEAR ROUND CARNATIONS

Carnations and pinks(dianthus) come in all shades of colour from white through pink, red, orange, yellow and mauve. Some are single bloomed, others multi-headed, some large, some small, some pure colours, some mixed, some striped, some frilled and many have a magnificent fragrance.

Carnations flower perpetually throughout the summer months and, once established, a carnation bed is left to flower for up to 5 years. As with Chrysanthemums, artificial lighting and heating conditions can be installed to adjust the flowering season and so produce blooms all year round.

CARNATIONS

Trends

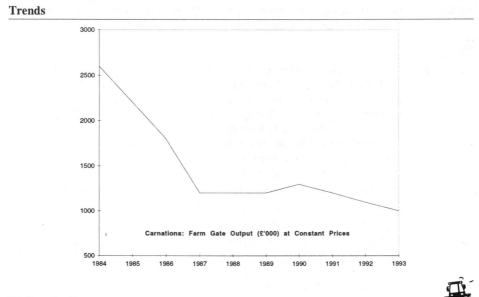

Carnations: Farm Gate Output (£'000) at Constant Prices

Husbandry Summary

Varieties	Sim types.
Medium	Border soil. Sterilisation by sheet steaming.
Environment	Carnation beds erected after border preparation. Irrigation drip lines installed. Capital installations given 5 year write off period. Blueprint schedules for temperature regimes: Sept - Oct 10°C, Nov 9°C, Dec 7°C, Jan 9°C, Feb10°C, March 11°C, April-Aug 12°C.
	960 sec heating oil used. 17.48 x 1000 litres per 0.1ha to maintain temp. regimes.
Nutrition	Blueprint base dressings. Liquid feeds via drip lines to blueprint. Watering requirements: allow 600 x 1000 litres per 0.1 ha.

Production Cycle

Late Sept	Plant out rooted cuttings 45 plants per sq. m of bed at 15cm x 15cm. 28,570 plants per 0.1 hectare. Artificial lighting used to increase daylength during periods of short daylight hours to maintain photoperiodic response.
Crop health	Biological control of the main pests is practised. Sticky cards also used for Aphid control. Predatory species are introduced into crop as pests (White Fly, Thrip, Spider Mite) build up. If unsuccessful approved compounds used (Diazatol, Captan, Iprodione, Pirimicarb).
Harvesting	Blooms hand cut into wraps of 20 stems. 12 wraps per non returnable cardboard box.

FLOWERING POT PLANTS

An enormous range of delightful flowering plants are available in pots, many of which will flower perpetually for long periods in the home or conservatory throughout the year. Amongst the most popular are Begonia, Azalea, Celosia, Cyclamen, Geranium, Impatiens (Busy Lizzie), Saintpaulia (African Violet) and Chrysanthemum. Growers organise production of these plants to meet seasonal demand, depending on variety and space available in the glasshouse ie. 'spot pot crops.' Pot Chrysanthemums will be described in detail as an example of a popular flowering pot plant.

POT CHRYSANTHEMUMS (SPOT POT CROP FOR CHRISTMAS)

Special dwarf varieties of Chrysanthemum have been cultivated to grow as pot plants. These are also treated with growth-regulators to retard growth. 'Spot pot crops' are carefully scheduled to market at specific times e.g. Christmas. As for the cut flower varieties, pot Chrysanthemums are subjected to artificial lighting and heating conditions in order to achieve this.

Trends

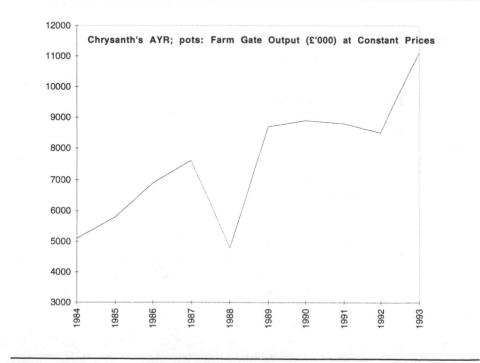

Chrysanth's AYR; pots: Farm Gate Output (£'000) at Constant Prices

POINSETTIAS

Husbandry Summary

Varieties	Princess Ann and other coloured sports.
Medium	Proprietary potting compost (loamless).
Environment	Blueprint schedules for temperature regimes. Maintain minimum night temperatures of 15°C 4 weeks after potting. Reduce by 2-3°C after 4 weeks. Ventilate at 21°C. 960 sec heating oil used. 10.73 x 1000 litres per 0.1 ha to maintain temp. regimes.
Nutrition	Additional feed of 50kg per 7000 pots Ammonium nitrate. 40kg per 7000 pots Potassium nitrate. Watering requirements: Allow 120 x 1000 litres per 7623 pots/0.1 ha.

Production Cycle

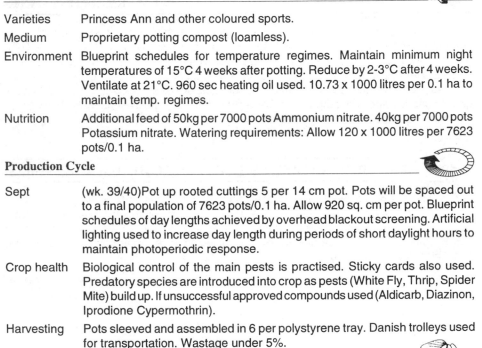

Sept	(wk. 39/40)Pot up rooted cuttings 5 per 14 cm pot. Pots will be spaced out to a final population of 7623 pots/0.1 ha. Allow 920 sq. cm per pot. Blueprint schedules of day lengths achieved by overhead blackout screening. Artificial lighting used to increase day length during periods of short daylight hours to maintain photoperiodic response.
Crop health	Biological control of the main pests is practised. Sticky cards also used. Predatory species are introduced into crop as pests (White Fly, Thrip, Spider Mite) build up. If unsuccessful approved compounds used (Aldicarb, Diazinon, Iprodione Cypermothrin).
Harvesting	Pots sleeved and assembled in 6 per polystyrene tray. Danish trolleys used for transportation. Wastage under 5%.

SPECIALIST POT PLANTS - POINSETTIAS

This crop is grown specifically for the Christmas market.

Husbandry Summary

Varieties	Ria, Annette, Hogg. Red, pink and white bracted varieties are available.
Medium	Peat based loamless compost.
Environment	Maximum temp. recommended 20°C, 18°C during initiation. As bracts develop an 18-20°C regime, with a reduced temp. (16°C) to promote bract colour whilst hardening off prior to despatch.
Nutrition	Modern systems feature mobile aluminium growing benches with automatic watering and feeding systems. Blueprint nutritional programmes inject N, P, K and Mg into the irrigation lines.

FOLIAGE PLANTS

Production Cycle

Jan	Place order for rooted cuttings with propagator.
Aug	(Week 30-34) Rooted cutting inserted in 14cm pots. 10cm are used for specific customers. With modern benching utilisation is 85-90%. Plant population 8,000 per 0.1ha. (i.e. 7600 pots grown). Growth regulators applied (Cycocel) 4-6 applications.
Sept - Oct	Space pots to final stand. Maintain routine feeds and watering regimes. Apply crop protection programme : biological control of the main pests is practised. Predatory species introduced into crop as pests (White Fly, Thrip, Spider Mite) build up. Sticky cards also used.
Dec	Weeks 48-51 are the peak harvesting and marketing weeks. The crop is generally packed in cardboard boxes in 6's. Polystyrene trays are used. Each pot is sleeved. Direct sales (ex nursery, van) common. The wholesale market is also used. % pot wastage is minimal.

FOLIAGE POT PLANTS

These plants are grown for their interesting leaf shape, colour or habit. Most require warmth during the Winter and collections of foliage pot plants are becoming increasingly popular in homes and offices as they need minimal care and are long-lasting. The range is vast, from massive rubber plants to dainty little ferns. Leaves are often striped or variegated, some upright, others trailing in habit.

Trends: All Pot Plants

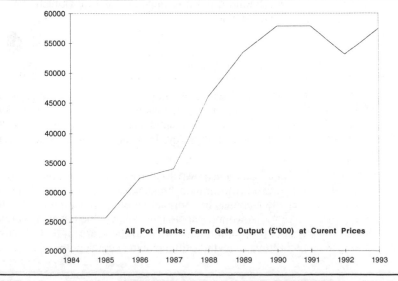

All Pot Plants: Farm Gate Output (£'000) at Current Prices

BEDDING PLANTS

Husbandry Summary

Varieties	Typically Ivies, Palms, Rubber plants (Ficus spp.), Rhoicissus and Cissus spp., Yucca, Caladium, Chlorophytum and Tradescantias. Many others including Sansevieria, Dracaena, Scindapsis, Monstera, Tillandsia
Medium	Proprietary composts, or self mixed loamless composts from peat, sand etc. Base fertilisers added during mixing process.
Environment	A range of growing environments, depending on species. For year round production minimum night temps. of 10 ° C in winter months (Nov - April). For many species humidity has to be high, requiring careful ventilation during hot weather. 35 sec heating oil used. 15 x 1000 litres to be budgeted.
Nutrition	Blueprint base dressings. Liquid feeds via spray lines may be necessary. Watering requirements: allow 160 x 1000 litres per 0.1 ha

Production Cycle

Propagation	Rooted miniplugs bought in from specialist propagators. Potted into 13cm (13F) pots.
Growing on	26 pots/sq.m with an 80% utilisation gives 11,800 plants/0.1ha. Large producers using mobile irrigation gantries to water crop. Overhead sprinkler lines or automatic aluminium troughs with fertigation units used. Mobile benching common to maximise area utilisation and keep labour costs down.
Crop health	A range of approved products are used to control the pests and diseases (Pirimicarb, Cudgel, Diazinon, Benomyl, Iprodione, Aldicarb used). Sticky cards used for pest control.
Marketing	Direct delivery via van sales to major customers (often Garden Centres) or ex nursery sales. Polystyrene 6 pot tray units handled by Danish trolley. Individual pot labelling essential.

SUMMER AND AUTUMN BEDDING PLANTS

'Bedding plants' is a very loose term used to describe plants which provide a temporary seasonal display of colour in borders, patios and hanging baskets. Many are annuals, which complete their life cycle within a year. Annuals are classified as either hardy, being able to cope with cold conditions in early spring, or half-hardy, less robust plants which need protection from frost.

There are simply thousands of plant varieties grown for sale as summer bedding plants, in the greatest range of colour, size and fragrance imaginable. All are raised under protection in similar conditions. Some biennials are popular for autumn planting, either to flower throughout the winter e.g. winter-flowering Pansies, or to flower the following spring e.g. Polyanthus, Wallflower, Myosotis (Forget-me-not). Bedding plants are marketed either as a collection of plants in strips or trays or as individual plants in small pots.

BEDDING PLANTS

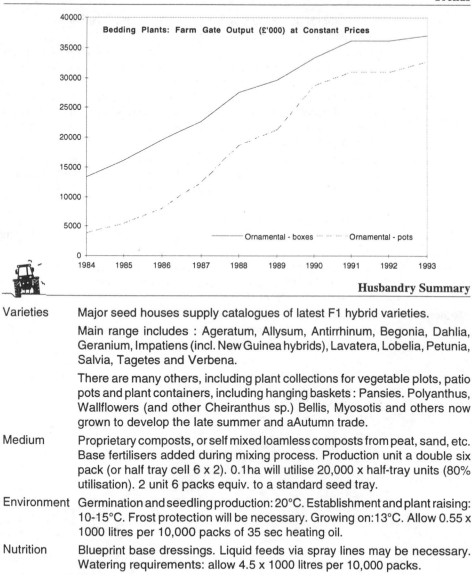

Bedding Plants: Farm Gate Output (£'000) at Constant Prices

Ornamental - boxes ·········· Ornamental - pots

Husbandry Summary

Varieties	Major seed houses supply catalogues of latest F1 hybrid varieties.
	Main range includes : Ageratum, Allysum, Antirrhinum, Begonia, Dahlia, Geranium, Impatiens (incl. New Guinea hybrids), Lavatera, Lobelia, Petunia, Salvia, Tagetes and Verbena.
	There are many others, including plant collections for vegetable plots, patio pots and plant containers, including hanging baskets : Pansies. Polyanthus, Wallflowers (and other Cheiranthus sp.) Bellis, Myosotis and others now grown to develop the late summer and aAutumn trade.
Medium	Proprietary composts, or self mixed loamless composts from peat, sand, etc. Base fertilisers added during mixing process. Production unit a double six pack (or half tray cell 6 x 2). 0.1ha will utilise 20,000 x half-tray units (80% utilisation). 2 unit 6 packs equiv. to a standard seed tray.
Environment	Germination and seedling production: 20°C. Establishment and plant raising: 10-15°C. Frost protection will be necessary. Growing on:13°C. Allow 0.55 x 1000 litres per 10,000 packs of 35 sec heating oil.
Nutrition	Blueprint base dressings. Liquid feeds via spray lines may be necessary. Watering requirements: allow 4.5 x 1000 litres per 10,000 packs.

BEDDING PLANTS

Production Cycle

All programmes geared to supply from April - July. Late summer and autumn programmes now significant .

Propagation — Specialist seeding lines enable full mechanisation. Seeded trays, often mini-modular trays for mechanically transplanting into double 6 trays, stood in germination rooms at 20-25°C depending on cultivar. Large producers are fully mechanised. Hand pricking-off still practised by many growers, especially with small quantities or poorly germinated batches. Individual tray labels inserted prior to standing down. Underfloor cable heating common in specialist producer units.

Growing on — Depending on the season; temperature regimes gradually reduced from 15-10°C prior to standing outside to harden off. Early production may have to be covered with floating fleece covers to protect from frost. Mypex floor covering common on standing out areas. Large producers using mobile irrigation gantries to water crop.

Overhead sprinkler lines or hand watering maintain optimum growing conditions.

Crop Health — A range of approved products are used to control the pests and diseases (Pirimicarb, Thiram, Diazinon, Benomyl, Iprodione, Heptenophos). Sticky cards used for pest control.

Marketing — Direct delivery via van sales to major customers (often Garden Centres) or ex nursery sales. Double 6 tray units handled by Danish trolley. Collection from nursery floor or standing areas labour intensive.

OUTSIDER'S GUIDE

FINANCIAL INFORMATION

Item	Cut Flowers			Pot Plants		Bedding Plants	
	AYR MUMS*	Natural season MUMS	Carnations	Flowering incl. MUMS*	Foliage	Trays	Pots
Production & Marketing							
Hectares	68	143	9	130	31	22 million units	90 million units
Number of producers	<300	n/a	<20	<50	<30	250-400	-
Av. unit size (est. ha.)	1.45	1.45	1.45	1.45	1.45	1.45	-
Average yield (per ha.)	1,300 - 1,500 boxes (20 wraps) [a]		9,000 wraps (1wrap=20 stems)	10,500 x 6's	11,000 x 6's	10,000 - 11,000 trays	6,500 - 7,000 x15's
Marketing channels	Van sales direct from the nursery, wholesale markets, garden and plant centres, some supermarkets, local authorities (parks & gardens), special mail order					Van sales, ex nursery, wholesale markets, garden and plant centres, some supermarkets, local authorities, special mail order	
Investment Considerations							
Typical investment (£/metre[2])	30-60[b]	30-60[b]		30-60[b]	30-60[b]	10-15[d]	10-15[d]
Minimum size of unit (ha)	1 - 1.5	1 - 1.5	1 - 1.5	1 - 1.5	1 - 1.5	1 - 1.5	1 - 1.5
Lead time to first crop	10-12 weeks	7 months	2-3 months	3-4 months	2-3 months	2-3 months	
Production cycles thereafter	3.3[c]		continuous May - Sept	continuous	continuous	yearly	yearly
Cycles per year	4.3[c]		continuous over 5 years	4.3	continuous	1-2	1-2
Rotational details	steam sterilisation necessary		steam sterilisation necessary	grown on raised benches			

* MUMS are chrysanthemums
a 1 wrap holds 5 stems
b Typically Venlo glass structure. Heating systems/boiler; £25000 /ha, pipework: £80,000 /hectare, thermal screen: £20,000 /hectare, potting machine: £10,000., precision drill: £5000
c Influenced by temperature and day length
d Polythene tunnel or multispan

SUMMARY

GROSS MARGINS

	CUT FLOWERS		POT PLANTS		BEDDING PLANTS	
Enterprise Item	AYR MUMS	CARNATIONS	FLOWERING AYR eg. MUMS	FOLIAGE	TRAY UNITS	POT UNITS
Example variety	Snowdon Hurricane Pink Gin Delta	Sim types	Princess Ann and sports	Various	Tagetes Ageratum Verbena Salvia	Various F1 Hybrids
OUTPUT						
Yield per 0.1 hectare	1,400 X 20 wraps (wrap=5stems)	9,000 wraps (wrap=20stems)	10,500 X 6's	11,000 X 6's	9,500 packs	6,600 X 15's (tray=15pots)
Price/unit of sale (£)	25.00 per box (box=20wraps)	25.00 per box (box=12wraps)	6.00 per tray	3.00 per tray	2.50 per unit	5.25 per tray
Enterprise output (£/ha)	**35,000**	**18,750**	**63,000**	**33,000**	**23,750**	**34,650**
VARIABLE COSTS (£) - Production						
Fertilisers	450	230	250	200	30	60
Sprays	600	50	1560[a]	300	100	150
Fuels & power[b]	2,500	1,800	2,500	1,600	750	70
Water	150	200	165	80	20	60
Sundries	200	1,340[c]	200	250	750[d]	125
Plants, seeds, pots, compost	5,600	3,500	14,250	3,500	2,650	11,200
Subtotal (£)	**9,500**	**7,120**	**18,925**	**5,930**	**4,300**	**11,665**
VARIABLE COSTS (£) - Marketing						
Casual labour, grading & packing	1,467	2,644	1,800	3,700	300	750
Packaging	2,100	160	3,500	400	-	1,500
Commission and handling (12 - 15%)	5,250	2,250	12,600	4,900	-	5,197
Transport	2,380	100	8,400	1,350	-	3,500
Subtotal marketing (£)	**11,197**	**5,154**	**26,300**	**10,350**	**300**	**10,947**
Enter output (£ / ha)	35,000	18,750	63,000	33,000	23,750	34,650
Total variable costs	20,697	12,274	45,225	16,280	4,600	22,612
Gross margin (£/ha)	**14,303**	**6,476**	**17,775**	**16,720**	**19,150**	**12,038**

a   includes special growth regulators
b   heating oil, electricity, gas, paraffin
c   includes £1,100/annum charge for fixed costs of carnation beds
d   casual labour

Gross margin

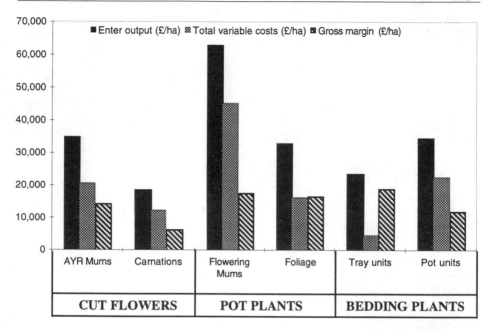

NOTES

SPECIALIST SECTORS

G: HARDY NURSERY STOCK

OUTSIDER'S GUIDE

HARDY NURSERY STOCK

There is an enormous range of different varieties of hardy (ie frost resistant) plants grown in nurseries. Most are long-lived and intended for eventual permanent sites where good root systems can be established.

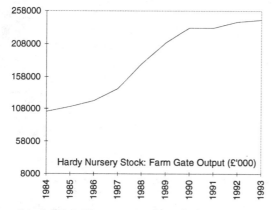

Hardy Nursery Stock: Farm Gate Output (£'000)

Many of these are now sold in individual containers, rather than bare-rooted. Some growers specialise in field grown plants particularly where soil conditions are favourable, others specialise in container plant production; usually a mixture of containerised field grown stock, and container grown plants (where the plants spend their entire life in containers up to the point of sale). The propagation of plants and production, up to the stage of initial small container potting, is increasingly being undertaken by specialist nurseries.

FIELD GROWN

Field grown nursery plants are discussed under three categories: (a) Herbaceous, (b) Shrubs, (c) Trees.

(A) HERBACEOUS

In field production, plants are 'lifted', 'split', and then either sold direct to the retail customer as 'root wrapped', or sold in a similar bare root condition to other nurseries for containerising. Some nurseries field grow to build stock, each year lifting and potting a certain number for their own wholesale container production. These are usually sold to garden centres, although the size of both the landscape and local government markets are expanding due to the increasing popularity of herbaceous plants.

Because of the cost effectiveness of 'division' on a field scale, as a method of propagation, this group of plants is quite different to any other. Obviously a high quality soil is required, together with a good water supply for regular irrigation. Sales are very seasonal due to the natural appearance (or lack of it) of most plant material during the autumn and winter. Sales are restricted in the main to spring and summer, which is convenient as lifting and potting is done during the winter. Plants range enormously in size and may be sold individually root wrapped, or occasionally sold in containers as large as 10 litres.

SHRUBS

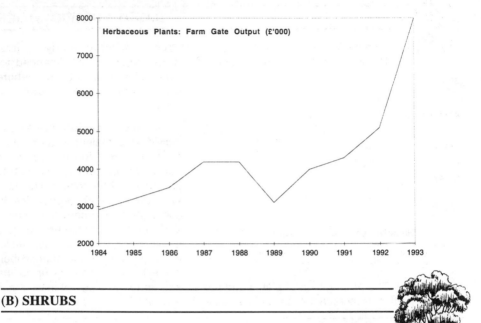

Herbaceous Plants: Farm Gate Output (£'000)

(B) SHRUBS

This is a limited market and is mainly used to produce plants which are sold in large numbers and therefore need to be inexpensive. Examples are Hawthorn and Privet.for hedging. Most shrubs today are propagated vegetatively then container grown; very few are field grown then containerised.

There is a slight improvement in this market at present due to the anti-peat lobby promotion of the Peat Free Charter. Local government in particular finds it very difficult to secure good quality supplies of container grown stock produced peat free. This is a situation which is likely to be short-lived. The market for field grown mature specimens is extremely small. A market for field grown stock is likely to prove difficult to obtain.

Obviously the soil type is crucial for this kind of production so land prices are likely to be at a premium. No allowance has been made for irrigation costs due to the unknown water source. Clearly a natural source would be cheapest, however some nurseries do exist without any. Their location within the country is the major influencing factor.

OUTSIDER'S GUIDE

Trends

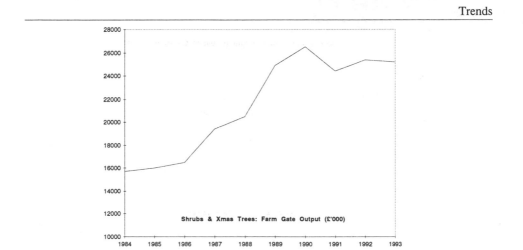

Shrubs & Xmas Trees: Farm Gate Output (£'000)

Probably some of the most popular shrubs sold are roses. Again, some are container-grown but field production is still significant, so the details will be used as an example of a field grown shrub.

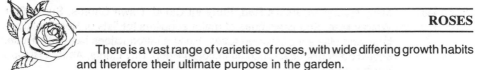

ROSES

There is a vast range of varieties of roses, with wide differing growth habits and therefore their ultimate purpose in the garden.

Bush roses are divided into two groups: Large flowered(Hybrid tea) and Cluster flowered(Floribunda). Both types can also be grown as standards on a tall stem, giving the appearance of a small tree. These are usually displayed in beds and borders often grouped to give splendid masses of colour and fragrance as they flower freely throughout the summer.

Some varieties, similar to the wild rose, are used for hedging eg. Rosa Rugosa, and ramblers or climbers, having a vigorous growth habit, are ideal for covering pergolas, walls and fences. Miniature strains of roses are now being successfully bred which are increasingly popular for planting in pots on patios where their root growth is restricted. The colour choice with all roses is enormous; some are pure, others mixed, some flecked or the petals edged in contrasting shades. Some buds are close set, others open right out to reveal the centre, some are highly scented, others are not.

ROSES

Trends

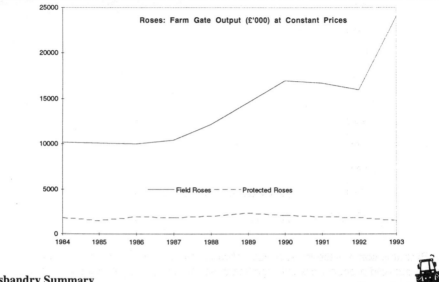

Roses: Farm Gate Output (£'000) at Constant Prices

——— Field Roses — — — Protected Roses

1984 1985 1986 1987 1988 1989 1990 1991 1992 1993

Husbandry Summary

Varieties	Many favourites: Alec's Red, Fragrant Cloud, Dawn Chorus, Super Star, Whisky Mac. See catalogues of major suppliers for lists of Rose cultivars, large and clustered flowered roses. Recent introductions like Patio Roses should be considered, such as Little Bo Peep, City Lights, Angela Rippon, Festival and Penelope Keith.
Soils	Well drained medium loams preferred. Windbreaks either natural or artificial may be necessary on very exposed sites.
Nutrition	Following soil analysis and dressings of N,P, & K to raise indices to level 3, apply annual dressings of 75kg N, 75kg P and 75kg Kper Ha. Additional top dressing with 30kg N may be necessary in growing season.

Production Cycle

1st year

Autumn	Fallow treatment to site selected is recommended. Application of Glyphosate for perennial weeds (couch grass, thistle, bindweed etc.). Deep subsoiling in both directions prior to ploughing, cultivations, base dressings of fertiliser etc. Some rose growers grow on ridges or on raised beds to assist lifting and budding.
Feb	In year 1 of production cycle suitable rose rootstocks are planted. 5-8mm stocks in 80-85cm rows, spaced about 17-20cm in the row. Mechanical

planters are used. Plant population approx. 60,000/ha. Residual herbicides applied post planting. Some hand weeding may be necessary. Stocks should be kept clean using crop protection pesticides such as Dimethoate, Bupirimate, Oxycarboxin and Myclobutanil.

July - Aug   Rootstocks 'T' budded with selected cultivars and held in place using rubber patches. Budwood taken from mother plants on nursery, or bought in as appropriate. Royalties will be paid on varieties registered under plant breeders rights.

2nd year

Feb - Mar   Rootstocks headed back and herbicides should be applied.

Mar - Sept   Maintain crop protection programme: Mildew and Black Spot are the main diseases, Aphid and Caterpillar the main pests. Materials as for Year 1.

Apr   Trim crowns of stocks to improve shape.

Oct   Prior to lifting the bushes are topped using specially adapted machines for mechanical defoliation. At harvest the crop is undercut, lifted, graded and despatched. Expected grade out 65-70% grade 1, 20-25% grade 2, the rest are unsaleable. Most bushes sold bareroot.

(C) TREES

A wide variety of trees are grown in nurseries, many being propagated by grafting and budding, while others are grown from seed or by taking hardwood cuttings.

Usually 'Transplants' or 'Whips', i.e. very young trees, are purchased which are planted out in rows, supported by a cane and then pruned throughout the next 18 months to 2 years to form a good standard tree. Unlike the container production, sales period is limited to the winter period only. Irrigation is on a field grown scale, like agricultural crops, when provided, avoided if at all possible due to costs. Good ground preparation is the main precaution (incorporation of Farm Yard Manure at 50 tonnes/ha against dry conditions.)

Compared with many other plants, the maturity of trees takes much longer and so they are prepared and grown in the nursery on a 2-5 year cycle before being ready to transplant to the final positions. Considerable investment is then tied up in space over a long period which must be reflected in the eventual selling price.

Some trees are slow-growing, others faster, some have a great potential size, others are comparatively 'neat' in habit. Trees can be chosen for the splendour of their leaves, fruits, flowers or perhaps just their interesting shape and form, some being evergreen, others deciduous.

The selection is vast and a general guide is given for details of production, rather than a specific example being chosen. Popular species include: Acers (Maples), Malus (Crab Apples), Prunus (Flowering Cherry).

TREES

The figures are for 'standard tree' production. This is a larger market than container trees because trees are cheaper. A market does exist for much larger field grown trees, these are usually marketed as 'root balled'. This requires expensive specialist equipment.

Trends

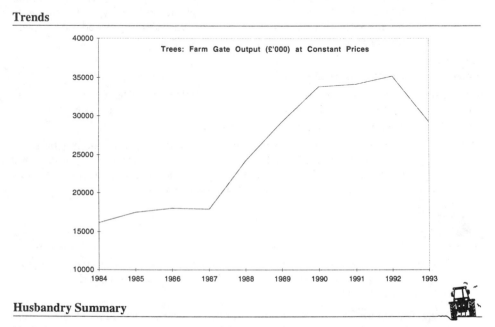

Trees: Farm Gate Output (£'000) at Constant Prices

Husbandry Summary

Varieties   A very wide range of cultivars are grown, including Acer, Prunus, Malus, Sorbus, Salix, Tilia. Many are propagated by grafting and budding, others from seed or hardwood cuttings.

Soils   Well drained medium loams and brickearths preferred. Frost free Grade 1 soils ideal. Permanent windbreaks such as Poplar and Alder are used to maintain optimum growing environment. Irrigation is desirable (to apply 70-90 mm per annum). In some areas rabbits are a serious problem. It is recommended that sites are rabbit proofed with appropriate fencing materials.

Nutrition   Heavy dressings of bulky organic manure recommended. 100 tonnes/ha of farmyard manure if available. Following soil analysis base dressings index 3's, annual dressing of 70-80kg N, 75kg P and 75-80 kg K per ha in 1st year. In 2nd year apply 180kg N, 80kg P and 80kg K per ha. Thereafter 100kg N per ha applied.

Production Cycle

1st year   If the selected site has a history of perennial weeds then a years fallowing is recommended. The applications of Glyphosate in mid summer onwards, followed by deep subsoiling, ploughing and cultivations prior to planting out rootstocks.

Feb   Plant out graded rootstocks mechanically using a slit trencher. Plant populations vary, an average being 92.5cm x 44cm in blocks of 12 rows, giving 20,000 to 30,000 plants per hectare. Headlands and pathways require 15% of area. Herbicides applied to maintain weed free conditions: Propyzamide and Paraquat used. Some spot treatments and/or hand weeding may be necessary.

Mar - June   Maintain crop protection programme using pesticides against Aphid, Caterpillar and Red Spider Mite. Certain cultivars are disease susceptible and will require fungicidal sprays.

July - Aug   Rootstocks are chip budded in the field and tied with polythene tape or rubbe bands. Buds should be sourced from healthy stock material, preferably virus tested from approved health schemes. By late August (or 6-8 weeks from budding) poly tapes released by cutting.

2nd year
Feb - Mar   Head back stocks. Any failed buds grafted over in early spring (allow 12-15%). All budded stocks caned with 2.5m bamboo canes ready to tie in new growth. Top dress with 100kg N per 20,000 trees. Apply annual herbicides (Propyzamide and Paraquat as appropriate).

Maintain full crop protection programme. Apply irrigation to maintain SMD under 10 mm for optimum growth. Tie in new growth to canes with proprietary taping machine e.g. Maxtapener.

Nov - Feb   Head off whip growing up cane to form primary branches. If tree has feathered, some shaping, trimming up or cutting of primary laterals required. Some cultivars are harvested at this stage.

3rd year +   Depending on the cultivar, maintenance repeats itself until the tree is of a saleable size. Periodic undercutting of the root system is vital in helping to develop a more compact and fibrous rootball which aids lifting and transplanting. Final trimming and training carried out.

Harvesting   In the summer prior to the winter liftingseason, a stock list is created of the various cultivars. Where batches are to be lifted, mechanical undercutting carried out in early autumn. At onset of leaf-fall, lifting, trimming and bundling prior to despatch carried out. 70-75% of trees lifted to minimum specification, depending on cultivar.

SUMMARY

FINANCIAL INFORMATION

Item \ Enterprise	Herbaceous*	Shrubs Field	Roses - bush	Trees - Field
Production & Marketing				
Total UK hectares	1000	150	787	4000
Estimated producer numbers	250	35	n/a	150
Average unit size (ha)	2	3	13-14	5
Plant density (N/ha)	66,000 a	55,000 a	60,000 a	30,000 a
Marketing channels	Garden centres & landscaping, amenity.		Garden centre amenity, mail order, supermarkets	
Investment Considerations				
Typical investment (£ /ha)	15000 b	500 b	900 c	1000
Minimum size of unit (ha)	1	2	2	2
Lead time to first crop (years)	1	1	2	2
Production cycles thereafter	n/a	n/a	n/a	n/a
Cycles per year	1	1	0.5	0.5
Rotational details				

* The nursery described is one which propagates in open ground and then containerises the plants for wholesale.
a Allow for 10% mortality due to disease and winter losses.
b Assumes 50:50 split field area and container site
c This assumes the land is rented. Items include normal requirements for an intensive arable farm under 100 ha. For land purchase add £5,000 per hectare.

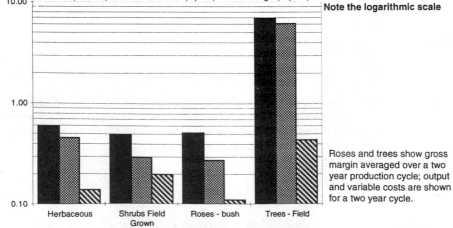

Note the logarithmic scale

Roses and trees show gross margin averaged over a two year production cycle; output and variable costs are shown for a two year cycle.

OUTSIDER'S GUIDE

Gross Margins

Item	Enterprise	Herbaceous	Shrubs Field Grown	Roses - bush	Trees - Field
Example variety		Various	Various	Large/cluster flowered	Various
OUTPUT					
Yield /ha (= Nºplants/ha)		60,000	50,000	50-55,000	27,000
Unit Price / plant (£)		0.60	0.50	0.50	7.00
Enterprise output		**36,000**	**25,000**	**27,500**	**189,000**
VARIABLE COSTS - PER PLANT - Production*					
Fertilisers		-	-	-	-
Sprays		0.10	0.05	0.01	0.45
Pots		-	-	-	-
Canes, ties, labels		-	-	-	-
Photo label		0.05	0.04	0.04	0.15
Stock costs		0.10	0.10	0.10	3.50
Consultants		0.01	0.01	0.01	0.02
Casual labour		0.20	0.10	0.12	2.00
Sub total production costs		**0.46**	**0.30**	**0.28**	**6.12**
Gross margin (£/ plant)		0.14	0.20	0.11 per annum (for 2 years)	0.44 per annum (for 2 years
Gross margin (£ / ha)		**8,400**	**10,000**	**7,700 per annum (for 2 years)**	**11,880 per annum (for 2 years)**

* Not including irrigation system or land.

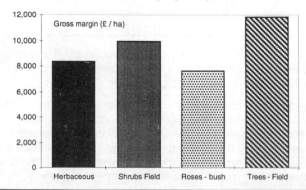

CONTAINER GROWN

CONTAINER GROWN PLANTS

Container grown plants provide a popular and convenient method of marketing a wide variety of nursery stock. Most garden centres and retail outlets are then able to sell products all year round rather than restricting the sale of various species to the appropriate seasons for lifting and planting. Roots remain undisturbed during movement and the appropriate irrigation and nutrition programmes can be easily applied at any time. Plant material is sometimes field-grown to transplant size and then potted up and grown on in containers. A whole range of nursery stock can be grown in this way.

Constituents of container composts vary widely, and in recent years nurseries have sought to move away from peat, which still forms the base material of most composts. Other substrates which are often mixed into peat-based composts include : Perlite, Rockwool, sand, grit and bark. The most popular peat-free alternatives are composted bark and coir.

Trends

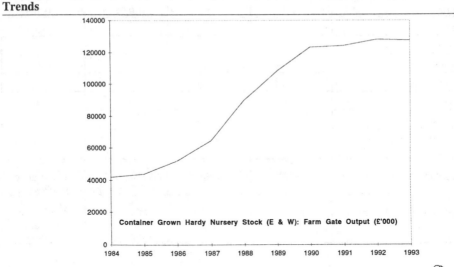

Container Grown Hardy Nursery Stock (E & W): Farm Gate Output (£'000)

(A) SHRUBS

The crop described is a common, easily grown shrub in a 3 litre rigid container. Most nurseries would propagate their own rooted cuttings, and then pot them onmay be several times before final sale.

The example given is for a nursery which buys in the rooted cuttings/ small plant liners then pots and grows them on. Liner prices could be expected to be about three times the price of a rooted cutting, but production time could be shortened to as little as four months. Shrub prices vary considerably depending on rarity. The shrub described is common and therefore very cheap. Unusual shrubs could be expected to fetch up to three times the price or even more in exceptional circumstances such as rare grafted plants.

CONTAINER SHRUBS

Husbandry Summary

Varieties	A wide range of plants are grown in this way and some of the techniques apply to the production of conifers as to the production of both deciduous and evergreen shrubs. Examples include : Elaeagnus, Deutzia, Philadelphus, Viburnum, Griselinia, Berberis, Forsythia, Hebe, Weigela, Olearia, Pittosporum and many others. Much of the broad information also applies to container grown ornamental trees and container grown perennials, heathers and alpines (with specific modifications in propagation and cultivation according to genus and species).
Soils	Container composts used. Containers are usually stood out on firm, well drained bases which are covered with a permeable woven plastic membrane sheet such as Mypex. Alternatives are sand or gravel beds. Good drainage essential. Irrigation is usually by overhead sprinkler but sand beds allow the watertable to be controlled by a simple cistern system, sometimes referred to as Efford beds. Good windbreaks are essential and both natural and artificial can be used. Beware of overwintering pest hosts in some natural species e. g. Poplar.
Nutrition	As recommended by HRI Efford the container compost mix should have 75% peat, 20% pine bark and 5% lime free sharp grit, 36kg Magnesian limestone, 4.5 kg of fritted trace elements (WM255) and 43kg of Osmocote 18:11:10 incorporated per 19-20 cubic metres of compost mix.

Production cycle

July +	Rooted cuttings are put into 7-9 cm pots (now called liners) from July-Oct and protected from low temperatures through the winter. Pot thick spacing on 1.5m beds : approx. 42.5 sq. m required for 5,000 pots. The propagation method and time of year is very specific for each cultivar, with some requiring specific bottom heat temperatures and growing regimes.
March +	Rooted cuttings or 'liners' raised in propagating area within nursery or bought in from specialist suppliers.
March - May	Liners are potted into 3 litre pots ; large growers have potting machinery and often automatic modular liner transfer to pots. Potted cultivars are assessed for susceptibility to frost damage and protected if necessary, then stood out on sand beds or standing areas. Some species require shaded conditions, and many 'softer' cultivars are grown on under plastic tunnels. Low tunnels are widely used to accelerate growth and shorten the production cycle. Caution must be exercised that plants do not become too 'lush' or 'soft' so increasing susceptibility to pests and diseases. Approx. area required: 210sq. m per 5000 3 litre pots outdoors on 2.5m wide beds, spaced at 25 cm centres Pathways will occupy 25% additional area. If 2 litre pots used,165 sq. m required at 18 cm spacing. Spacing is important and must

CONTAINER TREES

allow access to adequate light and water so that plants develop a natural, bushy habit.

April +
Routine weed control is essential (Oxadiazon e.g. Ronstar used). Chemicals incorporated into compost for Vine Weevil control, Pithium and Phytophora. Insecticides or natural predators used for Aphid, Caterpillar and Red Spider Mite control.

June +
Many cultivars have new growths pinched or pruned to encourage a bushy plant to improve sales. Maintain full irrigation programme to prevent pots drying out. Allow 200 x 1000 litres per 5000 pots. Top dress if required (35 kg 7:7:7 fertiliser per 5000 pots) or second application of controlled release type e.g. Osmocote. Any containers overwintered to sell 18 months from potting receive top dressing. Some cultivars potted on into 5 litre or 10 litre containers depending on sales strategy and customer requirements.

Harvesting
25-30% of plants will be ready for sale by autumn of 1st season, depending on range of cultivars grown. 70-75% will be saleable by the spring of the 2nd season. The proportion is totally linked to speed of growing and cultivars selected. Some may require growing on to the 2nd spring and 3rd autumn seasons. A usual grade out would be 65-70% 1st grade, 20% 2nd grade and 6-10% unsaleable. Printed and picture (where available) labels inserted prior to despatch to garden centres or major DIY centres (Homebase, B &Q etc). Danish trolleys are widely used to transport containerised shrubs.

(B) TREES

This is usually a crop of bare rooted trees bought in during the winter, potted, then stood in lines on a permeable plastic ground cover (which suppresses weeds). Occasionally containerised trees are grown on long, narrow sandbeds. The trees are supported by tying them to wires which are strung between stout posts. Each tree is usually given a 2m cane. The tree is fastened to the cane, the cane is attached to the wire.

Irrigation is mainly by 'Spaghetti Tubes' - a very fine bore irrigation to each pot - or by seep hose which is laid over the pots and literally seeps water through permeable stitching. Pruning is on-going throughout the production time.

A limited market for a high value crop. The detail given above (containerised shrubs) is for production in relatively small containers. Trees are also available in 25 litre, 50 litre, and 75 litre containers. The same production principles apply but specialist handling systems are required. N.B. Not all stock makes 'A' grade price. As much as 20% may be sold as 'B' grade and subsequently fetches a much lower price, or may even be dumped.

(C) ALPINE & HEATHER PRODUCTION

Both these crops require special attention and have different production requirements to anything else (including each other). For this reason it is not uncommon to find nurseries which specialise in these specific fields, although of the two crops, heathers are more easily integrated into a 'general' nursery production programme.

Because these plants are usually by nature quite small, it has evolved that they are sold as small plants. This means that the bulk of production focuses on 7, 8, 9 cm pots which are sold for a comparatively cheap price. The management of small plants is very intensive and so for this reason profit margins tend to be minimal. This is compensated for by the scope to turn out very large numbers. Heathers are now becoming more marketable in 1 litre and 2 litre containers, but profit margins remain narrow.

Plants in small pots need very level surfaces and a comprehensive watering system. Handling is also more expensive.

Note the logarithmic scale.

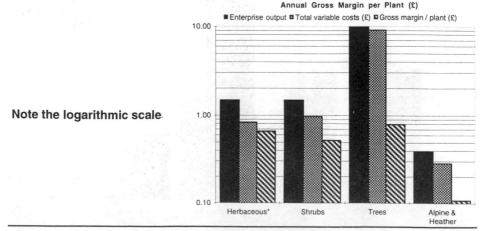

Annual Gross Margin per Plant (£)

■ Enterprise output ▨ Total variable costs (£) ▨ Gross margin / plant (£)

SUMMARY

FINANCIAL INFORMATION

Enterprise Item	Herbaceous*	Shrubs Container	Trees Container	Alpine & Heather
Production & Marketing				
Total UK hectares	1,000	3,500	2,000	200
Estimated producer numbers	250	275	200	160
Average unit size (ha)	2	5	4	1
Plant density (No./ha)	30,000 [a]	30,000 [a]	10,000	1,000,000 [a]
Marketing channels	Garden centres & landscaping, amenity.			
Investment Considerations				
Typical investment (£ /ha)	15,000 [b]	18,000	25,000	35,000 [c]
Minimum size of unit (ha)	1	1	2	0.2
Lead time to first crop (years)	1.25	1	0.75	0.5
Production cycles thereafter	n/a	n/a	n/a	n/a
Cycles per year	1	1	1	2
Rotational details				

*   The nursery described propagates in open ground and then containerises the plants for wholesale.
a   Allow for 10% mortality due to disease and winter losses.
b   Assumes 50:50 split field area and container site.
c   Level beds and good irrigation is essential.

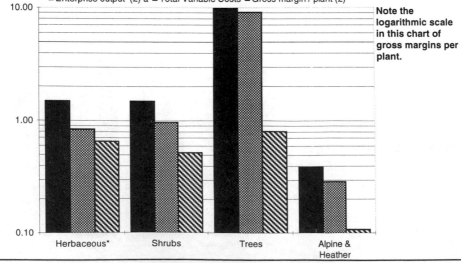

Note the logarithmic scale in this chart of gross margins per plant.

SUMMARY

Enterprise Item	Herbaceous*	Shrubs Container	Trees Container	Alpine & Heather
Example pot size	3litre	3litre	10-12 litre	8cm
OUTPUT				
Yield /ha (= Nºplants/ha) b	30,000	30,000	10,000	1,000,000
Unit price / plant (£)	1.50	1.50	10.00	0.40
Enterprise output (£) a	**45,000**	**45,000**	**100,000**	**400,000**
VARIABLE COSTS - PER PLANT - Production				
Compost &/or fertilisers	0.12	0.04	0.15	0.05
Sprays	0.10	0.15	0.04	0.03
Pots	0.12	0.12	0.80	0.025
Canes, ties, labels	-		0.15	
Photo label	0.05	0.04	-	0.035
Stock costs	0.20	0.10	5.00	0.05
Consultants	-	0.02	0.05	0.001
Casual labour	0.25	0.50	3.0	0.10
Total Variable Costs	**0.84**	**0.97**	**9.19**	**0.291**
Gross margin / plant (£)	**0.66**	**0.53**	**0.81**	**0.109**
Gross margin / ha (£)	**19,800**	**15,900**	**8,100**	**109,000**

* The nursery described is one which propagates in open ground and then containerises the plants for wholesale.

a Not including irrigation system or land.

b Selling actual plant thus only one production from each plant. No. per ha obviously influenced by chosen container size.

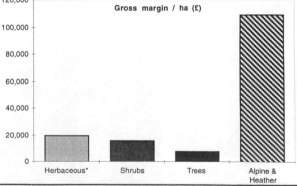

NOTES

SPECIALIST SECTORS

H: BEVERAGE CROPS

HOPS

BEVERAGE CROPS

British beers, wines and ciders are all well-established products, certainly for home-consumption if not exported in any significant quantity. There have been considerable changes in regulations and requirements for production of hops, vines and cider apples recently so these crops will each be discussed individually.

HOPS

The hop plant is indigenous to the temperate zones of Europe, America and Asia. The Dutch introduced hops to Britain in 1492, when beer was first brewed in place of ale. The inclusion of hops during brewing added bitterness, aroma and preservative qualities to ale, a taste which was not immediately approved of or accepted generally. However, as the art of brewing was perfected over the centuries, beer became a most acceptable British drink.

Different varieties of hops are grown for specific purposes, high alpha for bittering qualities, which are traded internationally, and fine aroma mostly used for traditional brewing. It is the choice of variety or blend of varieties used in brewing which produces individual brand preferences.

Hop plants are either male or female, male having seeds and female being seedless. Traditionally, seeded hops have been used in British brewing but now there is a demand for seedless hops for the increasingly popular lager market.

Traditional hop-growing areas are Kent, Sussex, Worcestershire and Herefordshire, all south of the critical latitude at which economic yields may be obtained. Hops are perennial and once planted are left undisturbed for between 10 and 50 years; the length of life of a 'hill' depending on the occurrence of pests and diseases, to which hops are susceptible. The crop is supported on permanent structures, 5-6 metres high, the plant growing rapidly during the spring, flowering in July and August and ripening ready for the hop harvest in September.

Harvesting used to be highly labour intensive but recent mechanisation has reduced this considerably. Hops are dried in 'oast-houses' on the farm and sold either whole or processed into pellets or extract. A Zentner is the universally accepted measurement for hops, being a weight of 50kg. The Hops Marketing Board existed from 1932-82. Following an EU directive, the industry was de-regulated and replaced in 1985 by English Hops Ltd. Since 1988 a number of individual growers and small groups have traded independently.

Alpha hop varieties are priced according to their alpha content, usually of the order of 10%, and traded on the commodity market. In 1994 prices paid were £24-26 per kilogram of alpha. Most is used in Britain for brewing but a small tonnage is exported for inclusion in lager brews.

HOPS

Aroma varieties, on the other hand, are priced according to hop pellet/extract weight. In 1994 prices ranged from £200 to £220 per zentner. British aroma hops have an established value on the international trading market and the future looks encouraging.

Hop growers benefit from an additional 'income aid' which is negotiated by the EU and paid annually. In 1994 the figure paid was £380/ha. Like most crops, hops are often grown on contract; a proportion is sold forward at a fixed price while some is held back for speculation.

Trends

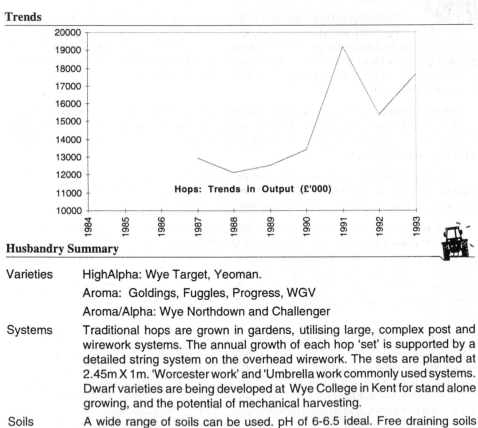

Hops: Trends in Output (£'000)

Husbandry Summary

Varieties	HighAlpha: Wye Target, Yeoman. Aroma: Goldings, Fuggles, Progress, WGV Aroma/Alpha: Wye Northdown and Challenger
Systems	Traditional hops are grown in gardens, utilising large, complex post and wirework systems. The annual growth of each hop 'set' is supported by a detailed string system on the overhead wirework. The sets are planted at 2.45m X 1m. 'Worcester work' and 'Umbrella work commonly used systems. Dwarf varieties are being developed at Wye College in Kent for stand alone growing, and the potential of mechanical harvesting.
Soils	A wide range of soils can be used. pH of 6-6.5 ideal. Free draining soils essential (soil borne Fusarium Wilt a serious problem of wet soils). The heaviest yields come from deep, brick earth type soils. The crop is responsive to irrigation. Modern gardens feature drip or low pressure irrigation emitters.
Environment	Sheltered sites are preferred. Perimeter windbreaks should be planted (Poplar, Alder) to improve microclimate and prevent crop damage during crop growth up the string system.

OUTSIDER'S GUIDE

Nutrition Soil analysis for N P K and Mg pre-planting. Repeat every 4-5 years. Annual dressings of 200kg N, 150kg K, 80kg P and 40kg Mg per ha are recommended. Apply N in 4-5 split applications through season.

Production Cycle

Jun - Oct In year prior to planting, apply herbicides on fallowed site to perennial weeds (Glyphosate). Deep sub-soil, plough, cultivate and apply N P K Mg fertilisers. Erect post and wirework system when good ground conditions. Top wires at 4-5m.

Oct + Plant large well rooted sets grown by specialist propagators in pots. Maintain weed-free garden, applying herbicides in small doses at regular intervals. Regularly spot treat for emerging weed seedlings, hand-pulling/ digging if necessary. After frosts, cut 'bines' to ground level to remove woody end-of-season growths.

Feb - Mar Insert hop screws at each set, and start stringing to wirework. A stringing pole is used, some garden workers still use stilts. As growth commences, remove 'rank growth' either selectively by hand or by strimming off new growths to encourage non-rank growths. 'Stringing' involves attaching 2-3 strings per set hopscrew on each hop 'hill' and running them up to the top wire system.

Apr - May 'Firsting' and 'seconding' carried out to ensure up to 6 shoots grow up the 2 strings at each hill. Final yield is directly linked to the fullness of the strings. 'Firsting' ensures new growths trained onto and around strings. Wind damage is a problem. 'Seconding' checks and corrects. Commence crop protection programme using air blast machines. Use Metalaxyl and Copper oxychloride, also Fosetyl-aluminium for Mildew control, at regular 4-5 day intervals.

May - Jun Apply Mephosfolan soil drench to hop sets to control Damson Hop Aphid. Keep use of broad spectrum insecticides to minimum to maintain high natural predator populations. 2-Spotted Red Spider Mite a serious problem-Phytoseilus and Anthocorids encouraged within garden to control mites. 'Rogue' hedgerows (dig out and destroy) near to gardens to eliminate male hops and prevent cross-pollination.

Sept Harvest. Usually 5-8 Sept for alpha varieties eg. Target. All bines cut down from wirework directly into field trailers and carted to 'picking machine'. Hops are plucked off bine mechanically, cleaned and transferred to oast for drying. Drying takes 8-9 hours at 180°F. The hops are compressed into 'pockets' or bales. Hop waste, the by-product, must be diposed of (burnt or used as a mulch) on site for reasons of hygiene and to prevent the possible spread of disease. It is of no financial benefit.

VINES

VINES

Although traditionally a very old enterprise, a revival in English wine making began in the 1950's and the wines are now well established. Many wines are of an excellent standard.

The British climate severely limits the areas suitable for growing vines, and most sites are restricted to land less than 100m above sea level along the southern coasts of England and Wales, also parts of Suffolk, Essex, Hertfordshire, Buckinghamshire and Berkshire.

Some vineyards incorporate their own winery, but this is not commercially viable under 5ha and smaller units sell their crop on to another winery which then adds transport costs. Vines are grown on a trellis system of which there are two main types, each type determining planting density and pruning system.

The first commercial harvest is possible in the 4th or 5th year after planting with 15-20 productive years to follow. Yield varies enormously depending on the season, from nil to 25 tonnes/ha in a good year. White wine is the most popular type ptroduced, 93.5% compared to 6.5% red.

English wine growers have been badly hit by recent EU regulations. Since 1991 there is a ban on new plantings of vines for table wine once annual production exceeds 2.5 million litres. However, there is no limit on 'quality' wine production, which must have a minimum natural alcoholic strength of 6%. English wines have to bear the same excise duty and VAT as imported wines, which is not the same in any other EU country. Since 1993 and the introduction of the Single European Market, British people are allowed to bring virtually unlimited amounts of wine into Britain duty-free. Consequently, English wine is not cheap and supplies only 0.5% of the home market.

Husbandry Summary

Varieties	Mueller Thurgau, Seyval Blanc, Reichensteiner, Schonburger
Rootstocks	Phylloxera resistant rootstocks are essential. Depending on soil type, medium rootstocks such as 904 and 50 can be used. For increased vigour (soil very poor or early ripening required) use 588 or 125AA.
Systems	Geneva Double Curtain (extensive): 2 parallel wires set out 1.5m from ground. Growths trained up and along wires, to cascade down with fruit.
	Guyot System (intensive): Series of 2-3 wires over 2.0m (first at say 0.4m). Fruiting growths trained onto and along all 2-3 wires.
Soils	A wide range of soils can be used. pH of 6-6.5 ideal. Free draining soils essential. The relationship between site, soil and microclimate is well recognised as the link to quality and volume in the major wine producing countries (together with the wine maker).
Environment	Gentle south facing slopes are preferred to drain cold air in spring (May frosts) and autumn (Oct frosts at harvest). Perimeter windbreaks should be

planted (Poplar, Alder) to improve microclimate, and vineyard 'paddocked' into 1-2ha blocks with internal Alder windbreaks. Vineyards should be protected from rabbits, hares and deer by a perimeter fence. A grass sward is recommended. Irrigation is desirable. Modern vineyards use drip emitters on low volume systems. Post and wirework to support a full field wiring system (see growing systems). Grape growers have to consider bird damage, and be prepared to net the crop at increased capital cost.

Nutrition   Soil analysis for P K and Mg pre-planting. Repeat every 4-5 years. Annual dressing of 70kg P, 150kg K and 40kg Mg per ha are recommended in 1st year. Apply 40kg P, 80kg K and 30kg Mg per ha in subsequent years.

Production Cycle

June - Oct   In year prior to planting, apply herbicides to perennial weeds (Glyphosate) on fallowed site. Deep sub-soil, plough, cultivate and sow over with grass.

Oct.   Apply N P K Mg fertilisers.

Nov - April   Plant new vineyard, using pot propagated varieties of known health status. For the Geneva Double Curtain system 2.4m x 3.7m (1126 vines/ha) used. For the Guyot System 2.0m x 1.5 m (3333 vines/ha). A black plastic mulch can be laid (1m x 5000m x 30 micron) to conserve moisture and eliminate competitive plants at the time of establishment.

April   Apply spring contact herbicides for annual/perennial weed control (Glyphosate and Paraquat) where necessary. Hand pull large weeds.

April +   Maintain full crop protection programme on developing shoots. Sulphur and Dichlofluanid used for Mildew and Botrytis control. In full production years a more comprehensive crop protection programme is required over 6-10 spray rounds using air blast sprayers. Vinclozolin, Chlorothalonil, Cypermethrin, Dimethoate and Fenarimol, plus Copper fungicide are the range of materials used.

May +   Insert 2.3m bamboo cane to each vine and tie in new growth.

May - Sept   Maintain soil moisture deficits within 25-50 mm using small droplet applicators or drip lines. Keep grass sward tightly mown.

June - Aug   Summer prune surplus growth off vines to direct energy into developing bunches. Tie in new shoots to develop full cropping mantle on wires.

Oct   Main harvest period. Pick into plastic buckets. Depending on variety and season (under UK conditions vines are very susceptible to variable yield) harvested yields will build up over 4 years to 5-10 tonnes/hectare. A best average yield would be 7.5 tonnes/ha. Each tonne yields 650-700 litres (866-900 x 75cl bottles) depending on season, pressing techniques and variety grown. Harvested grapes bought by the winery are valued at around £250 - £1000/tonne (related to variety and season). Winery operations include destrigging and milling/pressing, vinification, bottling, corking, labelling and casing prior to despatch. VAT and Excise Duty is charged on each bottle.

CIDER APPLES

Nov - March	Winter operations centred on pruning, tying in and shaping vines onto wire systems to achieve the highest volume of cropping vine/hectare. Laterals are shortened back to potential flower buds for flower quality and high yield.

CIDER APPLES

There are a wide variety of different apples grown for cider production which are reflected in the range of ciders available, from sweet to dry and still to sparkling. Manufacturers also range from small cottage industries to large multi-nationals.

Some cider orchards are specialist farms over 85 hectares (owned by Bulmers) but many are orchards within a mixed fruit farm of 20-30 ha. Cider apple production is mostly in the West Midlands, Herefordshire & Worcestershire, and the South West, Somerset & Devon.

Cider fruit orcharding has changed in the last two decades with the dramatic improvement in the marketing and consumption of cider. A considerable tonnage of low grade fruit from culinary and dessert apple growers is included for blending in cider or juice making. Apple juices are something of a fine art and are usually squeezed and bottled without additives or preservatives. Perry pears are treated in a similar manner to cider apples.

Fruit is generally milled and pressed mechanically to extract juice soon after harvest. Bulk fruit can be stored in cold store for a few months. The 'pomace' pulp is a waste product from milling, used for pectin making or cattle feed. Juice is pumped into fermenting vessels (wood or stainless steel) treated with Sulphur dioxide, yeast added and left to ferment. The type of juice, temperature and desired end-product will influence the duration of these processes. Once racked off into finishing vats, it will be bottled or kegged according to type of cider made. There are four main classes of cider - sharp, bittersharp, sweet and bittersweet.

Trends

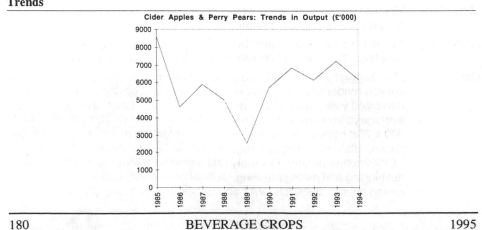

Cider Apples & Perry Pears: Trends in Output (£'000)

Husbandry Summary

Varieties	There are many traditional and local sweet and bittersweet varieties. Mid-season: Ashton Bitter, Ellis Bitter, Somerset Redstreak, Michelin, Yarlington Mill. Late season: Chisel Jersey, Dabinett, Brown Snout, Vilberie, Major. Cider manufacturers may specify their own varieties used in blending etc.
Rootstocks	MM106, MM111 and M25 are used to produce semi-dwarfing tree sizes.
Systems	Semi-intensive, hedgerow plantings now common. 3m X 6m (or 2.4m X 4.6m) give tree populations of 500-900/ha. Varieties with similar flowering periods should be planted near to one another, pollinators planted in single, complete rows. Biennielism (cropping every other year) is a problem with cider varieties. Growers try and reduce oversetting of fruit with chemical fruitlet thinners, and prune to maintain young 'wood' in the trees.
Soils	Reasonably free draining soils on sloping sites are required, especially to assist harvesting in late autumn (Oct/Nov) and may involve heavy harvest machinery. Orchard sites should be near hard roads to assist transport of fruit. Fruit washing facilities should be available.
Environment	Modern cider orchards require protection from wind and freedom from spring frost. Windbreaks (Alder, Poplar) should be planted to improve microclimate, and frost pockets in low lying land avoided.
Nutrition	Soil analysis pre-planting essential. Repeat every 5 years. Nitrogen rarely needed unless soils poor. Annual dressings of 10-25kg P, 25-35kg K, and 20-30kg Mg per ha, depending on annual yield (ref. biennielism). Foliar sprays: Magnesium sulphate (Mg), Urea (N), and Calcium chloride (Ca) are widely used.

Production Cycle

	New orchards are fallowed for 1 year prior to planting. Perennial weeds in full growth are sprayed with Glyphosate. Deep sub soil, plough, cultivate and sow over with grass. For hedgerow orchards burn out the herbicide strip prior to planting.
Oct - Nov	Plant new trees and tie to stakes. Well feathered trees are beneficial.
March - May	Apply spring herbicides and a straw mulch to conserve soil moisture and encourage tree growth.
March - Sept	Apply 7-14 day prophylactic sprays to control pests and diseases: Caterpillar, Aphid & Red Spider Mite are major pests, Scab & Mildew the primary diseases. Wood Canker should be cut out and the wounds painted.
May	In cropping years (2-3 years from planting) apply thinning agent (Carbaryl) if fruit set heavy.
Sept - Nov	Fruit harvest period. Hand harvesting carried out on smaller, younger trees. As orchards mature (after 5-7 years) mechanical aids used to harvest. Tree

SUMMARY

shakers are used to drop the fruit to the floor, which is then swept or brushed up with specialist equipment. A vibrating shaker arm clamps onto the tree trunk, vibrates for a few seconds to remove the fruit. Bins are either transported to the processor direct or tipped over into bulk tippers from a concrete loading area.

Nov - March   Tree pruning to maintain young growth, fill allocated space as quickly as possible. Remove diseased and broken branches.

FINANCIAL INFORMATION

Enterprise Item	Hops	Vines	Cider Apples
Production & Marketing			
Total UK hectares	3,396	1,054	4,000
Estimated producer numbers	150 - 200	500	150 - 200
Average unit size (ha)	4 - 20	2.5	5 - 10
Average yield (tonnes)	1.5	5 - 10	25 - 40
Marketing Channels	Grower co-operatives. English Hops Ltd. wholesale merchants.	Wineries producing mostly for export.	Bulmers, Merrydown,Showerings, Shepy, Westerns, Taunton Cider, independent merchants, Salvatori, Peter Hill, John Hill. ENFRU Ltd., SGT Ltd, Orchardworld, Aspall
Investment Considerations			
Typical investment (£ /ha)	15 - 20,000[a]	11,000-14,000[d]	1,000 - 2,000[c]
Minimum size of unit (ha)	4 - 20 [b]	5	5
Lead time to first crop (years)	2	3 - 5	3 - 4
Production cycles /yr thereafter	10 - 50	10 - 25	20 - 25
Cycles per year	1	1	1
Rotational details	Soil borne diseases, Verticillium Wilt	-	Apple Replant Disease thus rotate.

a   includes wire work and support poles, excludes vine stripper and drying oast

b   20 hectares for a 'stand alone' business. Most existing gardens part of a mixed farm.

c   Includes new plant establishment, including rabbit guards. Other fixed equipment is as other top fruit production - tractor, mower, and specialists harvesting machinery range from rear-mounted floor sweepers to shake and catch units (£8,000 +).

d   Addition of winery adds £50,000.

OUTSIDER'S GUIDE

GROSS MARGINS

Enterprise Item	Hops	Vines	Cider Apples
Example varieties	Wye Target, Wye Challenger, Goldings, Fuggles, Yeoman	Mueller Thurgau, Seyval Blanc, Reichensteiner, Schonburger	Michelin, Dabinett, Ashton Bitter
OUTPUT			
Yield per hectare (t)	1.50	5 - 10	35 - 40
Price/unit of sale (£/t)	4,000 [a]	250 - 1,000	80 - 100
Enterprise output (£)	**6,380** [b]	**1,250 -10,000**	**3,375**
Variable costs (£) - Production			
Fertilisers	200	1,150 [c]	50
Sprays	<750>	included in fertiliser	250
Herbicides	110	included in fertiliser	-
Fuels	150 [d]	included in fertiliser	Included in sprays
Direct casual lab	2,250 [d]	675-1,050	150
Harvest contractor	-	110	415 [e]
Sundries	185 [f]	included in fertiliser	150
Variable costs (£)	**3,495**	**1,935 - 2,130**	**1,015**
Gross margin (£)	**2,285**	**0 - 8,065**	**2,360**

a   Influenced by % alpha of hops grown.
b   Includes EU Income aid of £380
c   Total for ferts, sprays, fuels and sundries
d   For stringing and picking
e   Contract price £11 - £13/t
f   Sundries incl. pocket bales and string.

SUMMARY

Gross Margins

Note that in the gross margin chart below, there are two charts for vines - the worst and the best scenario. This is a highly variable crop. Yield varies greatly and this affects the total costs of casual labour required.

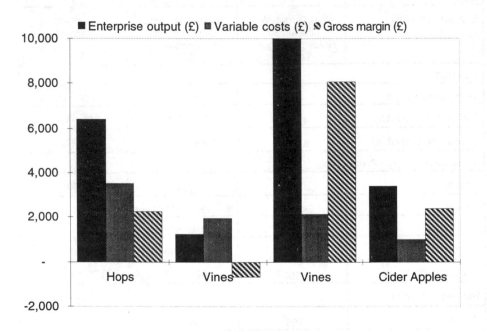

■ Enterprise output (£) ■ Variable costs (£) ⊠ Gross margin (£)

REFERENCE SECTION

I: REGULATIONS CONTACTS & TERMS

NOTES

REGULATIONS

EUROPEAN REGULATIONS AND THE INDUSTRY

Internal Market

With the completion of the internal market on January 1 1993, the European Commission has been formulating a substantial amount of legislation to ensure that each country's regulations relating to trade operate in complete harmony.

The Commission considers 'in principle' all national aids which distort trade and competition, or have a protectionist character to be incompatible with the Treaty of Rome. The main issues which concern the fresh produce trade are:

- ☛ Quality Control
- ☛ Labelling of Foodstuffs
- ☛ Food Safety
- ☛ Maximum Residue Levels
- ☛ Reduction of Packaging Waste
- ☛ Plant Passports
- ☛ Transport
- ☛ Metrication

These issues are still subject to debate, but at the time of going to press the position on each is as follows:

Quality Control

The Commission has tabled proposals for this new directive. The key debate relates to policing the system, with various alternatives proposed. Criteria to determine the maturity of apples and pears are also under discussion.

Labelling of Foodstuffs

This concerns labelling at retail level for pre and post harvest treatment. The Commission is awaiting a report on a survey amongst member states before tabling a proposal to the Council of Ministers.

Food Safety

The Community's proposals are unlikely to exceed the UK's existing Food Safety Act.

REGULATIONS

Maximum Residue Levels

The work of DGVI (Agriculture) in the field of harmonisation of pesticide residues (on fruit and vegetables) has advanced considerably. A first list of MRLs for 22 substances has been agreed. These MRLs came into force throughout the community at the end of 1993. A second list of MRLs is expected shortly.

Reduction of Packaging Waste

The current proposals under discussion are based on German packaging regulations. The proposals state that 10 years after the Directive comes into force, a minimum of 90 per cent of all packaging should be re-usable or recyclable.

Plant Passports/Phytosanitary Restrictions

An existing Council Directive is being modified to provide for the introduction of plant passports, and the ability to define certain areas of the Community as isolated zones, from which particular fruits and vegetables could be excluded. One such order has already been issued, banning certain citrus fruits from entry into Italy and Greece.

Transport

Many harmonising regulations are under consideration, but as yet no final proposal has been tabled.

Metrication

The final proposals to complete the metrication of UK industry are by way of implementation of the Units of Measurement Directive 89/617/EEC.

Sale of Bulk Fruit and Vegetables

From January 1, 2000 AD the use of the pound and ounce for the sale of all fruit and vegetables from bulk (i.e. not prepacked) will become unlawful. This will apply to all stages of distribution and it will be necessary for all traders to replace imperial weighing equipment with metric equipment by that date.

Weighing equipment for prepacking and making up packages or checking packages under the average system: non-automatic weighing machines used for weighing up goods in advance of sale generally ; those used for prepackaging fruit and vegetables in variable quantities and those used for making up or checking prepacks under the average system have to be in metric units from January 1, 1995.

Unit Pricing

Reference to imperial units (i.e. the pound) in the unit pricing of fruit and vegetables will not be allowed after January 1, 1995. All unit prices will have to be expressed as 'price per kg', etc.

DATA SOURCES

Further information - Regulations

Further information relating to Community regulations is available from the Fresh Produce Consortium, as it is published. Tel: 071-627 3391. Fax: 071-498 1191.

Statistical Sources

Agra Europe (London) Ltd.	Fruit and Vegetable Markets
Agro Business Consultants	The Agricultural Budgeting & Costing Book Nº 38
Food from Britain	Annual Report 1990/1991
Food from Britain	Food and Drink Trade Review 1993
Food from Britain	Food Focus 1
Food from Britain	Sector group report : Fruit , Vegetables
Food from Britain	The Food and Drink Trade Deficit report
Lynda Seaton (co-ordinating editor)	The Fresh Produce Desk Book 1994
MAFF	Basic Horticultural Statistics for the UK 1994
Nexus Business Communications Ltd.	The Grower
Nix, John, Wye College	Farm Management Pocketbook (1995)
Outsider's Guide to Agriculture	Crop Production 1995

Note that much information about specific enterprises is available through the relevant organisations listed under 'Contacts'.

CONTACTS

CONTACTS

1. Marketing Boards, Trade Centres and Related Organisations

Food From Britain	301 - 344 Market Towers, New Covent Garden, London SW8 5NQ Tel 0171 220 2144, Fax 0171 627 0616

2. UK Agricultural Training

Agricultural Co-operative Training Council	23 Hanborough Business Park, Long Hanborough, Oxford OX8 8LH Tel 01993 883577, Fax 01993 883576
Agricultural Training Board	Stoneleigh Park Pavilion, National Agricultural Centre, Stoneleigh, Warwickshire CV8 2UG Tel 01203 696996, Fax 01203 696732
National Poficiency Tests Council	National Agricultural Centre, Stoneleigh, Kenilworth, Warwickshire CV8 2LG Tel 01203 696553, Fax 01203 696128

3. UK Government Agencies

Apple & Pear Research Council	Bradbourne House , Stable Block, East Malling, Kent ME19 6OZ Tel/Fax 01732 844828
Intervention Board Executive Agency	Fountain House, 2 Queens Walk, Reading, Berkshire RG1 7QW Tel/Fax 01734 583626
Ministry of Agriculture, Fisheries and Food	Whitehall Place, West/East Block, London SW1A 2HH Tel 0171 27 3000, Fax 0171 270 8125

4. Wholesale Market, Fruit Buying and Merchant's Associations

British Fruit & Vegetable Canners' Association	6 Catherine Street, London WC2E 5JJ Tel 0171 836 2460, Fax 0171 836 0580
British Iceberg Growers' Association	133 Eastgate , Louth, Lincolnshire LN11 9QG Tel 01507 602427, Fax 01507 600689
British Independent Fruit Growers' Association	Broad Oak, Brenchley, Tonbridge, Kent TN12 7NN Tel 01892 722080
British Onion Growers' Association	The Packhouse Store, Ringmore Road, Southery, Near Downham Market, Norfolk PE38 0NJ Tel 013666 432
British Organic Farmers	86 Colston Street, Bristol, BS1 5BB. Tel 01272 299666, Fax 01272 252504
English Apples and Pears Ltd.	Brogdale Farm, Brogdale Road, Faversham, Kent ME13 8XZ Tel 01795 530666, Fax 01795 590177
English Quality Plum Growers' Association	Cotswold Orchards, Mount Pleasant , Worcestershire WR12 7JA Tel 01386 443142

CONTACTS

Farm Shop & Pick Your Own Association	NFU Offices, 22 Long Acre, London WC2E 9LY Tel 0171 235 5077, Fax 0171 235 3526
Flowers & Plants Association	Covent House, New Covent Garden Market, London SW8 9LY Tel 0171 738 8044, Fax 0171 622 5307
Food and Drink Federation	6 Catherine Street, London WC2B 5JJ Tel 0171 836 2460, Fax 0171 836 0580
Horticultural Development Council,	18 Lavant Street, Petersfield, Hampshire GU32 3EW Tel 01730 263736, Fax 01730 265394
Institute of Horticulture	P O Box 313, 80 Vincent Square, London SW1P 2PE Tel 0171 976 5951, Fax 0171 976 5951
Interflora British Unit	Interflora House, Watergate, Sleaford, Lincs NG34 7TN Tel 01529 304141, Fax 01529 304394
Leek Growers' Association	133 Eastgate , Louth, Lincolnshire LN11 9QG Tel 01507 602427, Fax 01507 600689
Mushroom Growers' Association	2 St Paul Street, Stamford, Lincolnshire PE9 2BE Tel 01780 66888, Fax 01780 66558
National Farmers' Union	22 Long Acre , London WC2E 9LY Tel 0171 235 5077, Fax 0171 235 3526
National Farmers' Union of Scotland	The Rural Centre, West Mains, Ingliston, Newbridge, Midlothian , Edinburgh EH28 8LT Tel 031 335 3111, Fax 031 335 3800
National Farmers' Union of Wales	Agriculture House, 23 - 25 Tawe Business Village, Phoenix Way, Swansea Enterprise Park, Llansamlet, Swansea, West Glamorgan SE7 9LB Tel 01792 774848, Fax 01792 774758
National Summer Fruits Association	c/o Elizabeth Browning, WFU Project Line, Crundalls, Matfield, Tonbridge , Kent TN12 7EA Tel 089 272 2803, Fax 089 272 3900
Northern Ireland Fruit Growers' Association	c/o Dermot Morgan, 90 Red Lion Road, Kilmore, Co Armagh, Northern Ireland BT6 18NU
Organic Growers' Association	86 Colston Street, Bristol BS1 5BB Tel 0272 299800, Fax 0272 252504
Processed Strawberry Growers' Association	c/o Tony Godfray, Croft Cottage, Panswell Lane, Leverington Common, Wisbech, Cambridgeshire PE13 5JS Tel 03945 410209
Royal Agricultural Society of England	National Agricultural Centre, Stoneleigh Park, Warwickshire CV8 2LZ Tel 01203 696969, Fax 01203 696900
Royal Horticultural Society	80 Vincent Square , Westminster , London SW1P 2PE Tel 0171 834 4333, Fax 0171 630 6060

CONTACTS

Soil Association	86-88 Colston Street, Bristol, Avon BS1 5BB
Special Salad Producers Association Ltd	133 Eastgate , Louth, Lincolnshire LN11 9QG Tel 01507 602 427, Fax 01507 600689

5. National Trade Associations

Asparagus Growers' Association	133 Eastgate, Louth, Lincolnshire LN11 9QG Tel 01507 602427, Fax 01507 600689
Brassica Growers Association	Potton Road, Biggleswade, Bedfordshire Tel 01767 312403, Fax 01767 317306
British Carrot Growers' Association	c/o Clem Tompsett, Whitehall Farm, Temple Road, Isleham, Ely, Cambs, CB7 5RF. Tel 01638 780087, Fax 01638 780056
British Food Export Council	301-344 Market Towers, New Covent Garden Market, London SW8 5NQ Tel 0171 622 0188, Fax 0171 627 5972
Commercial Horticultural Association	Links View House, 8 Fulwith Avenue, Harrogate, North Yorks HG2 8HR Tel 01423 879208, Fax 01423 870023
Fresh Fruit & Vegetable Information Bureau	Bury House, 126-128 Cromwell Road, London SW7 3ET Tel 0171 373 7734, Fax 0171 3733926
Fresh Produce Consortium (UK)*	103-107 Market Towers, 1 Nine Elms Lane, London SW8 5NQ Tel 0171 627 3391, Fax 0171 498 1191
Fruit Importers Association	62-65 Link House, New Covent Garden Market, London SW8 5PA Tel 0171 720 1387, Fax 0171 498 0058
Horticultural Trades Association	19 High Street, Theale, Reading, Berkshire RG7 5AH Tel 01734 303132, Fax 01734 323453
Worshipful Company of Fruiterers	Clerk: Commander Michael Styles RN, Denmead Cottage, Chawton, Near Alton, Hampshire GU34 1SB Tel 01420 88627, Fax 01420 88627

*The Fresh Produce Consortium brings together the fresh fruit, vegetable and flower industries of the UK into a unifying organisation for the development, enlargement and protection of the industry; including wholesalers, producers, packers, importers and exporters, plus retailers and distributors of every description. It represents the industry in negotiations, consultations and disputes with governmental and other official organisations in the UK, continental Europe and elsewhere worldwide.

OUTSIDER'S GUIDE

TERMS

'AYR'	all year round
1st earlies	particularly early maturing varieties, grown in 'early areas' e.g. Devon and Cornwall
2nd earlies	later than 1st earlies, but earlier than maincrops. Grown primarily in the northern and eastern counties
Annual	plant whose life cycle (germination, flowering, fruiting) takes place within the period of one year
Average farm gateprice	the average price received by growers for the crop. It is calculated from the monthly average wholesale market price which is a weighted average of the weekly prices published in the weekly MAFF Agricultural Market Report. Using appropriate factors to covert price per unit (e.g. bunch, box etc.) into price per tonne. Deductions are then made for wholesale commission market handling and carriage. This price is then adjusted to take into account the varying quantities and prices of output marketed through the different types of distribution outlets
Bedding plant	small annual flower plant used for bedding out
Biennial	a plant which completes its life cycle over two years, flowering and producing seed in the second year
Break crop	a non-cereal crop grown to act as a break to continuous growing of certain crops (e.g. between two cereals)
Calibration	graduation of spraying equipment so that it applies the desired amount over a given area
CIS	Commonwealth of Independent States
Coir	by-product of coconut processing, used as an ingredient of peat-free composts
Crop year	this relates to the nominal period of 1st June to 31st May during which the bulk of the crop is marketed
Cropped area	this is on the same basis as for the June Census i.e. it includes the area actually cropped and any adjacent headlands or ditches. This is generally known as "field" areas opposed to the planted area. For some crops such as lettuce, more than one crop (of lettuce) is harvested from the same area of land during the year. In this case that area would be added into the total as many times as it had been

TERMS

	cropped. For ornamental crops the area and quantity figures shown are those recorded by the Agricultural and Horticultural Censuses appropriate to the given production year
Cultural	produced in specially prepared media
Desiccation	spray applied to weeds - literally to dry them out and therefore kill them
Drill	sow seed
E.F.T.A.	European Free Trade Association
F.E.P.A.	Food and Environmental Protection Act 1985
Feathered whip	A tree in its second or third year of growth when the main stem has side branches developing
Fertigation	The practice of supplying fertilisers in the water supply
Fixed costs	costs which cannot readily be allocated to a specific enterprise on a farm, or will not vary with small changes in the scale/output of the enterprise
Forward contract	a sale of a commodity which is currently still being grown by the farmer, to his local merchant at an agreed price for delivery after harvest
Futures contract	this is the name for a forward contract to buy or sell a given amount and quality of a commodity at an agreed time in the future and at an agreed price. This is done through London Fox
FYM	farm yard manure
G.A.T.T.	General Agreement on Tariffs and Trade
Gross production	the product of the estimated gross yield and cropped area. It represents the maximum available supply during a crop year i.e. if all the crop was harvested and there was zero wastage
Gross yield	the average gross yield per hectare relates to the "field" and not the "planted" area. It is an estimate of the weight of crop available for harvesting from each hectare cropped during a single crop year. No deductions are made for the possibility that some of the crop may not be harvested nor for losses following harvesting
Growth regulators	chemical applied to regulate plant growth, usually to reduce height
Guide price	the EU Guide Price is set by the Council of Ministers at a level considered to be a fair return to the producers
H.S.E.	Health and Safety Executive
Half-hardy	plants not resistant to frost which can stand a certain amount of cold, so germination and subsequent growth is usually in a glasshouse

Harden off	to make plants which have been raised in green house become gradually more used to the natural temperature outdoors; traditionally cold frames were used for this
Heavy land	soil with an above average clay content (difficult to work down to a seed bed with machinery)
Herbaceous	plant which produces soft, non-woody growth, usually dying down in winter and producing new growth from basal shoots in spring
High clearance sprayer	spraying equipment designed to work in tall crops without damaging plants
Host	a plant which acts as a home for a pest or disease
Intervention	system of price support within the European Union based on buying into store surplus produce so taking it off the market to maintain market price at a pre-agreed level
Leaching	soluble nitrates moving down through the soil profile, possibly into drainage water
Levy	the fee charged by a board per hectare of crop grown
Loam	a medium textured soil containing a balance of sand, clay and silt
Lodge	crops bending over, making harvesting difficult
Lodging	the breaking of stems of cereals and grasses usually due to heavy rainfall and/or wind. This is often combined with high nitrogen uptake by the plant
Main crop	the greatest proportion of the UK crop grown to be stored in order to supply the market through the winter and spring until new crop is available
Malting	barley grown for brewing
Micro nutrients	elements required by plants in very small quantities
Micro-mole	unit of measurement for glucosinolate content
Mounted sprayer	sprayer, without wheels attached to the hydraulic lift of the tractor
Nitrogen index	an indication of residual nitrogen. This varies according to the previous crop
Nursery	place where plants are grown until they are large enough to be planted in their final positions
Organic produce	crops grown using natural fertilisers and not chemicals
Other soft fruit	this includes gooseberries
Output	output is the actual quantity that moved off the national farm and for which revenue was received. It is arrived at by reducing gross production by a wastage factor. It includes fruit sold for juicing
P.M.B.	Potato Marketing Board

TERMS

Packhouse	building used for grading, cleaning and packing produce of a farm, before it is sent to the customer
Perennial	term applied to plants which persist for more than two years
Pesticides	any chemical which is used to kill, control or diminish not just insects, but also weeds and diseases which challenge man, his crops, his domestic animals and his environment
pH	a measure of acidity or alkalinity. Range extends from zero to 14, pH 7.0 is neutral, below 7.0 is acidic.
Polygonums	the Latin name for a particular family of spring germinating weeds
Post-emergence	after the crop emerges
Pre-emergence	before the crop emerges
Prick out / off	to transplant seedlings from trays or pans into pots or flowerbeds
Protected crop	crop grown under some form of protection, such as in greenhouses or under polythene sheeting; in the UK, the main areas are in Guernsey and along the south coast; commonest protected crops are tomatoes, cucumbers, lettuces and mushrooms
PYO	Pick-Your-Own
Residue	what remains on the plant after spraying with pesticides
Rotation	growing of a series of crops in regular order to avoid exhaustion of the soil and build up of diseases
Seed treatment	chemicals applied to the seed before drilling often for crop protection purposes
Selective	choosing to affect certain parts only. For example, a selective herbicide kills weeds but leaves the crop relatively unaffected
Soil-acting residuals	substances remaining in the soil to act at a later date; for example herbicides that remain in the soil to kill weeds as they germinate
Soil-moisture deficit	(SMD) the difference between soil water gain and soil water loss
Species	plants of the same genus which may interbreed
Spot price	term used for the actual price of a commodity offered for sale on the open market on any given day
Spring bedding	bedding plants planted in October, seed sown in June and July. Plants grown as for Summer bedding but require less heating (e.g. Winter Pansies, Myosotis)
Spring crop	spring drilled crop
Standard	type of tree or bush where the stem is about two metres high, on top of which the head is developed. In UK orchards, standard trees have been replaced by bush varieties which are easier to prune, spray and harvest

Strip	thin punnet, usually four strips to a standard size carrying seed tray
Summer bedding	grown from seed and sown January to March
Swathing	crop left out to mature
Tenant's capital	farm assets normally provided by tenants and includes livestock, machinery, crops in store, stocks, work in progress, cash and other assets needed to run a business
Threshold	a level or incidence of infestation of a disease which justifies the use of control measures such as pesticides
Tillers	shoots from the base of a stem of cereal plants
Trace elements	elements required in very small quantities by plants but which are essential for the normal metabolism of the plant
Uruguay round	latest round of G.A.T.T. negotiations started in 1986 and due to have finished in 1993
Value of Imports	the value of a product at point of entry. It includes freight , insurance and all other cost charges and expenses incidental to the sale and delivery of the good to the port of place of importation in the United Kingdom
Variable costs	costs which can easily be allocated to a particular enterprise and vary directly with the scale/area of the crop grown - fertilisers, seed, sprays, casual labour, etc.
Varietal susceptibility	some varieties are susceptible to a particular herbicide product
Variety	type of cultivated plant - there may be several varieties for any particular species of plant
Volunteers	plants grown by natural propagation rather than having been planted
Wastage	in determining the wastage factor consideration is given to the amount of mature crop fit for sale but left in the field and ploughed in or damaged in weather, losses in grading storage (including any loss of weight in storage) and dressing after the crop has left the field and any of the crop which remains unsold due to lack of demand. Wastage does not include fruit sold for juicing and only relates to that part of the crop that attracted zero revenue
Wetter	added to pesticides or micronutrients to improve uptake through the foliage
Whip	a tree in its first year of growth when it is a single stem. See also feathered whip
Winter crop	autumn drilled crop
Working capital	assets required to finance the production cycle such as all variable cost items, plus labour, power costs etc.